The Battle of Chaldiran: The History and Legacy
Decisive Victory Over the Safavid Dynasty in Anatolia

By Charles River Editors

Battle of Kosovo, by Adam Stefanović (1870)

About Charles River Editors

Charles River Editors is a boutique digital publishing company, specializing in bringing history back to life with educational and engaging books on a wide range of topics. Keep up to date with our new and free offerings with this 5 second sign up on our weekly mailing list, and visit Our Kindle Author Page to see other recently published Kindle titles.

We make these books for you and always want to know our readers' opinions, so we encourage you to leave reviews and look forward to publishing new and exciting titles each week.

Introduction

A contemporary Ottoman depiction of the battle

The town of Caldiran (Chaldiran) in Turkey is home to about 60,000 people. On a plain close to the Iranian border, it it backdropped by the Armenian Ranges and very close to a Faultline, which has ensured it's suffered from seismic activity many times in the past. But in the early 16th century, it was the site of different kinds of faultlines, serving as a battleground between the region's two greatest powers as they clashed over politics and religion.

In terms of geopolitics, perhaps the most seminal event of the Middle Ages was the successful Ottoman siege of Constantinople in 1453. The city had been an imperial capital as far back as the 4th century, when Constantine the Great shifted the power center of the Roman Empire there, effectively establishing two almost equally powerful halves of antiquity's greatest empire. Constantinople would continue to serve as the capital of the Byzantine Empire even after the Western half of the Roman Empire collapsed in the late 5th century. Naturally, the Ottoman Empire would also use Constantinople as the capital of its empire after their conquest effectively ended the Byzantine Empire, and thanks to its strategic location, it has been a trading center for years and remains one today under the Turkish name of Istanbul.

In the wake of taking Constantinople, the Ottoman Empire would spend the next few centuries expanding its size, power, and influence on the way to becoming one of the world's most important geopolitical players. It was a rise that would not truly start to wane until the 19th century, and while its most memorable conflicts were fought against the Europeans, the course of Ottoman history was greatly impacted by events against the other major Muslim power in its region: the Safavid Empire.

Naturally, the two powers quickly took up the geopolitical positions of the old Byzantine and Persian Empires in the time before Islam and fought over much of the same territory, including Mesopotamia, the Caucuses, today's eastern Turkey and the Persian Gulf. Their first battle was fought in 1514, their first real war was fought from 1532-1555, and they continued to spar regularly until the early 19th century, when European colonialism forced them both onto the defensive. Echoes of these conflicts can be seen in the recent sparring between Iran and Turkey through proxies in Iraq and Syria.

On August 23, 1514 the two sides clashed at Chaldiran in a contest for hegemony over the Middle East, and the results have affected the Middle East ever since. Regrettably, few concrete details of the actual battle survive, a not uncommon obstacle when studying battles from the Middle Ages. However, the course of the conflict can be reconstructed from the politics of the time, knowledge of the characters involved, the contemporary records are available, and what followed the battle.

There is no lasting monument to the battle in Chaldiran on site, but there is on the Iranian side of the border, nearly 20 miles to the east near the village of Gala Ashaki. It consists of a domed tomb for a Persian general, Sayyed Sharif-al-Din Ali Shirazi, who fell in the battle. He was the chief religious cleric of Shah Ismail I, the first of the Safavid rulers of Persia and a leader who brought a monumental religious shift to the Middle East. Believing himself the "Shadow of God" and his chosen vessel, he set about transforming Persia and the globe through his fanatical religious militia, the *Qizilbash*. He meant to lead not only Persia but the entire Islamic world, but this vision was vehemently opposed by Sultan Selim I of the Ottoman Empire. Selim the Grim had fought tenaciously for possession of his throne, and he too believed himself chosen by God to rule all Muslims.

The battle is depicted in a magnificent painting in Sayyed Sharif-al-Din Ali Shirazi's tomb. In the foreground of the representation, Shah Ismail I of Persia leads his *Qizilbash* in a charge against the Ottoman cavalry, riding over the corpses of the slain. In the middle, Sultan Selim (who did not actually participate in the battle, though he was present) leads an almost leisurely advance toward the Persian cavalry, preceded by two Janissaries armed with axes. In the background, the Ottoman artillery delivers a barrage into the *Qizilbash*, who are falling or fleeing. It seems to be a chronological depiction of the conflict, and though the figure Ismail is clearly the centerpiece, there is no attempt to mask the fact that the battle was a catastrophic defeat for the Persians.

The Battle of Chaldiran: The History and Legacy of the Ottoman Empire's Decisive Victory Over the Safavid Dynasty in Anatolia examines the history of the belligerents leading up to the momentous conflict, what happened at the battle, and the aftermath. Along with pictures of important people, places, and events, you will learn about the battle like never before.

The Sunni-Shia Split

The roots of the animosity between the Ottomans and the Safavids could be traced almost all the way back to the establishment of Islam itself, many centuries before either empire was formed.

In the process of founding the religion of Islam, Muhammad had constructed around himself not only a potent new religious movement but also a powerful young state called the Ummah (the "Community" for lack of a better translation). Belonging to the Islamic faith also meant belonging to the Ummah, which was governed by its own laws and had many of its own institutions. In his own lifetime, Muhammad had ruled the Ummah through what sociologists call "charismatic authority," a term coined by Max Weber that is defined as "resting on devotion to the exceptional sanctity, heroism or exemplary character of an individual person, and of the normative patterns or order revealed or ordained by him." Hence, Muslims believe Muhammad ruled because he was uniquely chosen and endowed by God as the exemplar of all humanity, giving him a unique (though not perfect or infallible) ability to govern humanity. This was a holistic form of governance because the Prophet did not simply deliver God's words (what became the Holy Qur'an), nor did he simply pronounce upon court cases and create laws. He did all those things, but he also presented in his own person the embodiment of the best that humanity could aspire to. He was fully human, but the finest, most pious example that humans would ever produce[1].

One of the problems with charismatic authority, as Max Weber recognized and pointed out, is that charismatic authority is fragile because it cannot last beyond the lifespan of the charismatic individual without major changes. As a result, it is often difficult to create continuity after the death of a charismatic leader. Plenty of societies or movements have experienced collapse or massive upheaval after the death of a charismatic leader, such as France after Napoleon and the ancient world after Alexander the Great.

The process of converting a charismatic authority into a more stable, long-term form of government is called "routinizing charisma." In this process, the society attempts to keep some of the legitimizing elements of the deceased leader in place while also creating ways to choose new leaders. This can be agonizing, especially since new leaders rarely live up to or replace the one who has come before. That said, history has provided several successful examples, such as the Roman Empire after Julius Caesar, the Christian Church after Jesus, and the Islamic Republic of Iran after Ayatollah Khomeini.

The Ummah understood that once Muhammad died, he could not be truly replaced and that there would never again be a man like him. That said, the Ummah hoped to find a leader that was

---

1   "Max Weber's Conceptualization of Charismatic Authority: Its Influence on Organizational Research" by Jay
    A. Conger in *Leadership Quarterly* V 4, I 3-4, pp 277-288

still significantly superior to the ordinary man, and the most obvious candidates for superior people were the Prophet's family. Was there some way that the special qualities of Muhammad could be found amongst the members of his close family? Was there some special teaching or insight that Muhammad passed on to his family? Were Muhammad's teachings and the blessings of God only to be found within the Qur'an and the emulation of the life of the Prophet and therefore available equally to all Muslims? If there was something special about Muhammad, then special consideration should be given to the Prophet's family in the political life of the new Islamic state. However, if the leaders of the Ummah should be chosen based on their knowledge of the Qur'an, their piety, and their ability to administer and defend the community, then there was no need to turn just to Muhammad's family for leadership.

Ultimately, those who believed in a special place for the role of the Prophet's family became the Shias, while those who believed that all Muslims were equally capable in the eyes of God became the Sunnis. Even today, however, many rulers claim lineage to the Prophet as a form of legitimacy, including in Sunni states such as the modern Hashemite dynasty in Jordan.[2]

Upon Muhammad's death, the debate was between two individuals: Abdullah ibn Abi Qhuhafah (commonly known as "Abu Bakr") and `Alī ibn Abī Ṭālib ("Ali").

---

2   For the ancestry of the Jordanian Royal House, visit their official homepage:
      http://www.kinghussein.gov.jo/rfamily_hashemites.html

A 16th century depiction of Abu Bakr in Mecca

Both men were already eminent within the Ummah and featured prominently in the histories of the Life of the Prophet. Abu Bakr was the father-in-law of the Prophet and - like Muhammad - was a merchant based in the city of Mecca before Muhammad declared his Prophethood. He was outside Mecca traveling with a caravan as Muhammad first announced his new faith, and when he returned to the city, Abu Bakr was the first convert to Islam from outside Muhammad's own family. This was a major step because Muhammad called upon Muslims to abandon narrow clan ties for connection to the larger Ummah, and Abu Bakr served as one of the Prophet's closest advisors. While his daughter Aisha was married to Muhammad, since the Arabs were (and remain) patrilineal, this meant that Aisha entered Muhammad's family (male line), but it also meant Muhammad did not enter Abu Bakr's family. As a result, Abu Bakr is not considered to be a kinsman of the Prophet.

Ali, on the other hand, was family. The cousin of the Prophet on the male line, he was also married to the Prophet's most beloved daughter, Fatima. According to Islamic histories, Ali was born in the Kaaba, the sacred shrine at the heart of the holy city of Mecca, and he was the first man to convert to Islam upon hearing Muhammad's message. Like Abu Bakr, Ali had served as the Prophet's lieutenant, especially in military matters. Ali had regularly led the Muslim troops into battle.

A 16ᵗʰ century depiction of Ali leading soldiers in battle

When the Prophet died in 632, choosing Muhammad's successor was a decision ultimately made by the Sahabah, a term used for the body of individuals who had known the Prophet during his life (in English, it is often called the "Companions of the Prophet"). It is difficult from such a distance to say exactly why the Sahabah preferred Abu Bakr over Ali, but there are several plausible arguments, and it's safe to assume that even Abu Bakr's supporters would have had different reasons for their allegiance to him. One is that Abu Bakr was considerably older than Ali, and in the strictly hierarchical society of Medieval Arabia, age and experience were vitally important. There is an old Arab saying that men are not wise until the age of 40,[3] and Ali was only 32 or 25 (depending on which source on his birth one reads).[4]

Another possible reason for excluding Ali from the center of power may have been based on the fact he was a member of the Prophet's family. Early Islam was a religion that placed a great emphasis on egalitarianism, especially since the Prophet and the Qur'an called upon Muslims to reject their old ties of clan, tribe, and ethnicity. It may have been that the Sahabah wanted precisely to avoid creating a hereditary dynasty within the Prophet's family as a supreme rejection of the old clannishness[5].

Whatever the reasons, Abu Bakr was chosen to become "caliph," a shortened form of the title "Khalifat Rasul Allah" ("Successors to the Messenger of God"). The Caliph inherited all of the Prophet's political authority and much of spiritual power as well.

Since the election of Abu Baker in 623, there have been hundreds of individuals from close to a dozen dynasties that have claimed the Caliphate, but only the first four are widely considered by Sunnis to have inherited the true spiritual mantle of the Prophet. These four men, all of whom were Sahabah (Companions of the Prophet in his life), are called the "Rashidun" (or "Rightly Guided" Caliphs), and their government is referred to as the Rashidun or Patriarchal Caliphate (632-661).

After the Prophet's death in 632, the Caliphate controlled the Arabian Peninsula, which today consists of Saudi Arabia, Yemen, Oman, the United Arab Emirates, and Qatar, but it expanded during the Rashidun period with the conquests of today's Iraq, Syria, Israel, the Palestinian territories, Jordan, Persia, Armenia, Egypt, Cyprus, Lebanon, Azerbaijan, Kuwait, and Bahrain, as well as portions of Afghanistan, Turkmenistan, Turkey, and Libya.

However, it was also during this period that the division between Sunnis and Shias was taking shape. Initially, it consisted of a political division, with the proto-Shia as something akin to a loyal opposition; they supported the overall system of the Caliphate, obeyed the Caliph's rulings and were pious Muslims, but they believed that Ali was the better candidate and may have had strong opinions about the special place of the family of the Prophet in public affairs.

---

3   This is a widespread belief in Arab lands, and was confirmed by the fact that Muhammad's Prophethood did not begin until his fortieth year.

4   "The Caliphate" in *Islam: Faith, Culture, History* (2002). By Paul Lunde. DK Publishing.

5   *No God But God: The Origins, Evolution and Future of Islam* by Resa Aslan (2011). Random House

Succeeding to the caliphate in 634, Umar ruled until 644 and profoundly shaped the emerging Muslim state largely through his skill as a jurist and lawmaker. Under Umar, the Caliphate continued to expand, conquering the Levant, Egypt, coastal Libya and - crucially for the future history of Shias - the entire Persian Empire. Umar attempted some reconciliation with the extended family of Ali, but he still maintained Abu Bakr's position on Fatima's contested inheritance at the oasis of Fadak.

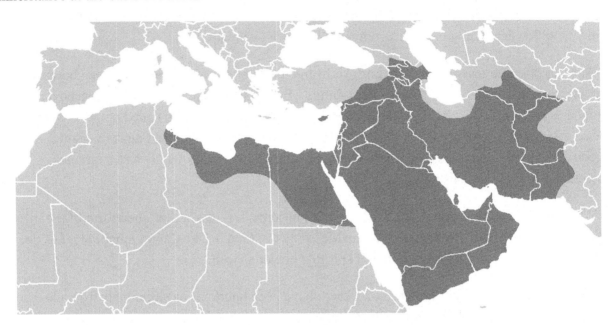

Mohammad Adil's map of the expansion of the Rashidun Caliphate

For the Sunnis, Umar has gone down in history as the greatest of the Faqih, an expert in "fiqh" (Islamic jurisprudence). During this period, the Ummah went through major changes as the number of Sahabah (Companions of the Prophet - those who heard Muhammad speak and had direct knowledge of his teachings) was decreasing both overall (as people like Abu Bakr died) and as a percentage of the overall population. This meant that the direct lessons of the Prophet and his example were becoming increasingly more difficult to teach, and as the Empire expanded, there was a greater need to apply Islamic law to an ever-growing number of cultural contexts. Umar and the scholars of his period began the process of collecting and codifying the Hadith (teachings of the Prophet) and creating a body of organized, universally-applicable laws for the new state[6].

In 644, Umar was murdered by a stab wound from a slave, and the fact that this slave was of Persian origin became a point of Sunni-Shia friction centuries later after Persia converted to Shi'ism under the Safavids. On his deathbed, Umar appointed a committee of six men to find his successor, and this committee included Ali and the eventual choice, Uthman ibn Affan. All six were part of the aging cohort of Sahabah and had been prominent political actors throughout the

6   *Islam: Faith, Culture, History* (2002). By Paul Lunde. DK Publishing. Pp 48-49

Prophet's reign and the succeeding caliphs.

The committee had to come to consensus, and according to legends, Umar ordered his son to kill any single member of the committee who held out against consensus. One of the six, Zubayr, backed Ali, and another, Sa'd ib Abi Waqas, supported Uthman. The remaining candidate/committee member, Abdur Rahman, withdrew from the running and was appointed arbiter. The final committee member, Talhah, was not present because he had been in a distant part of the empire when Umar died.

Eventually, the committee gathered before the Ummah at the Friday night prayers in the Mosque of the Prophet in Mecca, and when Abdur Rahman gave his support to Uthman, it forced Ali's hand. The committee announced it had reached a consensus, but Shias continue to maintain that Ali never accepted Uthman because he knew that the Prophet had appointed him as the only legitimate successor.

Regardless, upon his ascension, Uthman continued the military campaigns of his predecessor and pushed Islamic armies into Khorasan (today's northwestern Afghanistan), Balochistan (southern Pakistan), Armenia, and northern Africa. His rule lasted for 12 years, but while the first half of his reign was peaceful, the second half witnessed growing discord that eventually led to open revolt. The Shia argue that even in the time of Uthman, the later tendencies of the Sunni caliphs towards rule not as the first among equals but as dynastic monarchs was evident. Uthman had appointed his family members to governorships, accepted rich gifts, and used monies from the public treasury for himself, all of which flew in the face of the rigid egalitarianism of the previous rulers.

All of the discord culminated in 656 with the assassination of Uthman and unrest across the empire. The assassination itself was a dramatic event known as the "Siege of Uthman," which consisted of angry citizens/rebels from outlying areas converging on Mecca with a set of demands for Uthman. Central to their complaints was Uthman's appointment of his extended family as governors. The exact events are still unclear, but it is possible that documents were faked by his cousin Marwan (who would later be Caliph) that ordered the rebel leaders executed. Ali was called upon by Uthman to intercede, but his attempts at negotiations failed, so the rebels continued to besiege Uthman within his home. The siege was a slow-motion affair of many days and largely without open bloodshed - Ali was even able to bring water to the Caliph – but in the end, rebels led by Muhammed ibn Abu Bakr broke in and killed the Caliph[7].

Not surprisingly, the nature of these revolts and the assassination is clouded by centuries of assertions by Sunni and Shia, especially since the development of radical Wahhabi Sunni theology in the 19th and 20th centuries. The Wahhabis (who are discussed in much greater detail

---

7   "'Uthman ibn 'Affan" in *The Encyclopedia Britannica* accessed online at:
    http://www.britannica.com/EBchecked/topic/620653/Uthman-ibn-Affan

in the final chapter) argue that the decline of Islam is due to the corruptions of the true faith, in particular by the Shia, who they view as heretical. These theologians and historians argue that the Caliph was brought down by a Jewish figure named Abd Allah ibn Saba' al-Ḥimyarī, and that he was funded by external enemies of the Islamic empire to sow divisions within the faith and undermine the Caliphate. They argue that the theological roots of Shi'ism comes from this individual, who led a revolt movement that assassinated Uthman in order to put the corrupted Ali on the throne and end the Empire's expansion. The Wahhabis point to connections between some of the rebels and Ali, including Muhammed ibn Abu Bakr, who was Ali's adopted son[8] and became a general for him when he was Caliph.

Shia historians, on the other hand, claim that Abd Allah ib Saba' al-Ḥimyarī is a fictional character created to disparage the Shia by claiming that their theology is Jewish in origin. This is considered an especially damning charge after the creation of the state of Israel in 1948. Moreover, the Shias insist that Abd Allah ib Saba' al-Ḥimyarī was concocted to place the blame for the end of the Rashidun Caliphate on their betrayal[9]. Instead, they argue that the Caliphate lost its path when it appointed a figure other than Ali as Caliph in the first place, and that the creeping growth of this corruption could be seen in Uthman's increasingly monarchic tendencies.

In 656, Uthman's death finally made Ali the leader of the Caliphate, and respect for Ali and for his caliphate is the last point of historical commonality between the Sunnis and the Shia before their trajectories took them in different directions. Changes had swept the Ummah (community of Muslims); the Prophet had died 34 years ago, and the community of his Companions - the Sahabah - were vanishing and losing their control over social and religious life. Thus, Ali took over an empire in the throes of revolt but managed to hold onto power for the next five years.

Immediately after the death of Uthman, the rebel factions declared Ali to be their Caliph, but Ali turned them down at first. As a result, the rebels demanded a Caliph be appointed, so the remaining members of the committee that appointed Uthman and were in Medina - Ali, Talhah, Zubayr[10] - met together in the Mosque of the Prophet with others of the Sahabah. This committee eventually appointed Ali the new Caliph, but there would be debate among those involved, as well as historians, as to whether this was done willingly or by force. Either way, the events at Medina were not unchallenged by those opposed to Ali, and conflicting rumors spread like wildfire across the Empire about the nature of Uthman's death and the appointment of Ali. The opposition gathered around Aisha, the Prophet's wife, and then around Muawiyah, the second cousin of Uthman and Marwan and the governor of Syria in Damascus[11]. Another lesser faction was based in Egypt around the governor of that province, Amr ibn al-As.

---

8   The first Caliph, Abu Bakr, was his biological father.
9   For a summary of the evidence in the debate, read: "Authentic References and Case Research of ibn al Saba's Existence" accessed online at: http://makashfa.wordpress.com/2012/12/16/authentic-references-and-case-research-of-ibn-al-sabas-existance/
10 Sa'd ib Abi Waqas, was governing Persia at the time.
11 He was not, however, one of Uthman's nepotistic appointments as he had been given his position by Umar.

In one form or another, the First Civil War (called a "Fitna") consumed Ali's reign and ultimately brought about his death. Around him gathered a group of loyal followers who became known as the *Shī'atu 'Alī*, a term that means Party of Ali, and over time, "Shiatu Ali" became shortened to "Shia," the term that continues to be used today. Hence, it can be said that while the roots of Shi'ism go back to even before the death of the Prophet, the Shia become an identifiable political group upon Ali's succession.

The Rise of the Ottomans

The origins of the Ottoman Empire and the dynasty that founded it are surrounded by legends and mysteries. The mythology around Osman I and his closest family created an image of the dynasty, legitimizing their heritage and right to rule. While some of it surely is true, a lot of it may also be sheer exaggeration. Even the true origin of the Ottoman dynasty is heavily debated by modern historians. The general opinion is that the Ottomans descended from the Kayi tribe, a branch of the Oghuz Turks. This was never mentioned in any records actually written by the time of Osman I's life, but firstly 200 years later, which makes it a highly contested statement. Contemporaneous writers would claim Osman to be a descendant of the Kayi tribe to aggrandize him.

The Kayi Tribe was powerful, prosperous and played an important role in the Caucasus region, both at the time before Osman was born and for hundreds of years to come. To link the Ottoman dynasty with such a tribe would work as an incentive to keep up good relations with the actual Kayi tribe, and also inflate the story about how the Ottoman dynasty descended from power and political influence. It would also support the inherited right of the Ottoman dynasty to rule the area. Though this may never be clearly settled amongst historians today, we do know that Osman's family was one of many Oghuz Turkish people originating from what today is western Kazakhstan, just east of the Caspian Sea.

From there, the Seljuk tribe of Oghuz people moved southwest into Persia and founded their empire, slowly moving west towards the Byzantine Empire. When the Seljuk Empire disintegrated, many smaller states were formed all over Anatolia and Osman's father Ertugrul was a ruler of one of them. Legend has it that Ertugrul and his army of 400 horse-borne fighters accidentally came upon a battle between two foreign armies. Heroically he decided to intervene and support the side currently losing. With his help, they turned the battle and won. Ertugrul learned that he had been fighting on the side of the Sultan of Konya, from the capital of Rum, against the invading forces of the Mongolian armies.

As a reward for his actions, he was handed a piece of land in northwestern Anatolia, centered around the town of Sögut. The truth in this story is again under debate since it wasn't written down until much later. There is no clear evidence of how Ertugrul came in possession of the lands he ruled or what his relationship was with the Sultanate of Rum. All we can say for sure is that this became the embryo of the Ottoman Empire as Ertugrul settled down, got married and later also had a son, Osman. This happened sometime in the middle of the 13th century, but the exact date of Osman's birth was never recorded.

During the years of Osman's childhood, his father was the chief of his given lands but also subordinated the Sultanate of Rum. When Osman was 23, his father died and Osman inherited the title and power Ertugrul had earned. It was now nearing the end of the 13th century and the Sultanate of Rum, as well as the whole Seljuk Empire, was disintegrating. The rise and expansion of Osman's territory came more or less as a natural consequence, replacing one power with another. It was a gradual process going on for generations of the Ottoman dynasty and Osman's early conquerings were only a fraction of how large the empire would become. The necessity of expansion was in later years explained with the spreading of the Muslim faith. The truth behind this is a contaminated topic among modern historians and hard to verify. Islam is no longer considered to be a driving force for either Ertugrul or Osman. Ertugrul was not a Muslim, but many claim Osman's religious father-in-law converted him to the faith. The story of how Osman became a devout Muslim is of importance to the Ottoman legacy. It includes a prophecy where God himself appoints Osman and his descendants to glory and success. This was in later centuries used to legitimize the continued rule of his heirs. It was also Osman who named the whole empire and the following dynasty, still alive today. Osman is the Arabic version of the Turkish Uthman, or Athman, which scholars believe was Osman's real name. His name changed into Osman under influence from the Arabic and Persian Islamic culture, to signal his transcendence into a Muslim. Whether or not Osman was religious he decided to expand into Byzantine territory and kept peace with his Turkish neighbors. Until the actual dissolution of the Seljuk Empire, the Ottoman dynasty did not fight other Turkish tribes.

To try to pinpoint the descent and origins of the Ottoman dynasty and Osman himself is more or less impossible today. The sources are highly contaminated with propaganda like factoids about Osman's persona, his heroic actions and the constant success of his ambitions, written at the height of the Ottoman Empire hundreds of years after Osman's reign. There are hardly any actual records from his childhood and we know very little about his early years of conquest. Probably because at the time being, Osman's father and family were not considered particularly mighty or influential. Thus, the lack of contemporaneous writings implies the falsehood of the anachronistic records speaking of Osman's visions and also of his father's heroic intervention against the Mongol army. Anatolia consisted of many beyliks at the time, as well as different alliances between tribes from all over Eurasia, Eastern Europe, Middle East and as far away as Central Asia. The number of interconnections and movements between the different tribes are uncountable, which makes it harder to factually pin down the true origins of Osman's ancestors. Whoever the ascendants of Osman truly were one can safely say that his descendants, using his very name, would be well-known to historians and civilians for many centuries.

As stated above, Osman was born as the son of a chief in northwestern Anatolia, in the town of Söguk sometime around the middle of the 13th century. The exact year has not been confirmed by any reliable sources, but 1258 is usually mentioned as most likely. His mother is presumed to be Halime Hatun, but even this has not been securely confirmed, and hardly anything is recorded of who she was. It is known that Osman grew up in his hometown with two brothers but until his marriage to Mal Hatun there's not much information of his whereabouts. As the firstborn son of a local chief, Osman was aware of the fact that he would someday inherit the position, and it is said he learned to ride and fight already as a child. The first story recorded by the 15th century historians of the Ottoman Empire is the one about how Osman became a Muslim. It was during a visit at his good friend Sheik Edebali's house, who was a very religious man, that he found the Quran. Osman became interested and asked his friend what this book was. His friend, who was an influential religious man in the community told him it was the holy book of Islam.

Osman lay awake that night, reading and reading until he couldn't keep his eyes open anymore. He fell asleep at the auspicious hour of dawn and then dreamed of a tree, sprouting from his navel with branches reaching all over the world. People in the dream were happy and the landscape was beautiful. When he woke up in the morning he told Edebali about the strange dream who in turn explained that because Osman had read the book so intensely and honestly, God had chosen him and his descendants to be blessed with glory and honor for many generations to come. Sheikh Edebali then gladly gave Osman his daughter Mal Sultana to marry and of their love, many poems have been written. The union of the two families benefited Osman greatly according to later sources because Sheikh Edebali was associated with very devout and ascetic dervishes. Though the dervishes didn't have any riches or power, their relationship to Allah would help benefit the Ottoman dynasty. The story of how Osman was the first in the family to actually become a devout Muslim was important to legitimize him taking over the remnants of the Seljuk Empire.

Osman's dream wasn't written down until almost 200 years later, a time when such a story would be of importance to keep the Ottoman Empire united. The story was valuable to the unification of separate Muslim emirates and gave Osman the right to conquer them.

After Osman had gotten married and his father had passed away, he was a full-fledged leader of the beylik, with a strategically important territory and prosperous family ties through his marriage. The stream of warriors and refugees made Osman a ruler of more people than his father, and with more people, more lands were needed. To expand at the cost of the Byzantine Empire was a logical solution, and it is estimated that he started his expansionist campaign in the year 1288. His first target was two nearby fortresses, Karacahisar and Eskişehir. A decade later, in 1299, he conquered the two larger towns of Yarhisar and Bilecik from the crumbling Byzantine Empire. He made Yarhisar the new capital of the beylik and declared independence from the Seljuk Empire.

By then, the central rule of the empire was weak and the popular Sultan had been forced to flee the lands a couple of decades earlier. In his wake, there was chaos and no strong ruling power.

The newly born independent state under Osman was organized as a strong central government on the same principles as the previous Sultanate of Rum. Though many people in the peripheries were opposed to Osman's rule, he quickly lightened the tax burden of his new citizens which assuaged them and changed the negative opinion of him. He needed to establish trust and loyalty amongst the people who are furthest from the capital to stabilize the borders, and the low tax strategy worked well. He was also the first chief in the area to mint his own coins which points to Osman's ambition of creating a larger organized political entity.

After the declaration of independence, Osman continued to expand both southwest and north into Byzantine territory aiming to control the whole area between the Sea of Marmara and the Black Sea. He conquered towns along the coasts and the poorly organized Byzantine armies were coerced to draw back towards the Bosphorus. In 1308 he captured the last city on the Aegean coast, Ephesus, and thus achieved his goals of dominating the region. His mounted forces used multiple creative military strategies for defeating the enemies around the countryside of Bithynia and fought in ever-surprising formations. During his last years in life, he also had good help from his sons, especially the oldest, the heir to the throne Orhan. After a whole life on the battlefields with his father, Orhan had learned and fully mastered the ideas behind Osman's tactics.

The last successful campaign of Osman was the siege of Bursa, though his son was left in charge and Osman himself didn't participate physically. Orhan showed tenacity and chose to lay siege to the city instead of attacking and conquer it forcefully. The siege was successful and the city surrendered after two of years under the threat of starvation. This was the last and most important victory of Osman I's expansion in Anatolia, not fully complete until the same year Osman died, 1326. After Bursa fell under Ottoman rule, other cities in the vicinity soon followed suit. It became the new capital under Orhan and an important staging ground against further expansion to the west.

The Battle of Pelekanon in 1329 was the first time the Byzantine armies met the Ottoman forces. The clash ended with a shattering defeat for the attacking Byzantines, although their numbers were larger and they possessed more experience from battle than the Ottomans. Contemporaneous sources explain the crushing win with the Byzantine spirit already being broken by the empire's civil struggles while the confidence of the arising Turks made them fight with more vigor and conviction.

The Battle of Pelekanon marks a significant turning point in the history of the region. The Byzantine Empire never again tried to reclaim the lost territories on the Asian side of Bosphorus and more or less left Nicea and Nicomedia to be besieged and later incorporated into Orhan's beylik. By 1340 Orhan had also annexed the beylik of Karasi which was the first time he had chosen to march towards Turkish neighbors. He did so because the chief had passed away and the two sons of the chief were currently warring against each other to claim the title. Many soldiers and civilians had already died when Orhan decided to intervene for the sake of peace. One of the brothers was killed and the other captured and Orhan now ruled four provinces. Most of the cities within the beylik were peaceful and many former Christians quickly embraced Islam without coercion. The region needed to be stabilized in order to build the strong state apparatus as the foundation of an empire. Orhan had put all of Bithynia and the northwestern corner of Anatolia under his control without much resistance from the population.

After his brother's death in the early 1330s, Orhan had the help of his two eldest sons Suleyman and Murad in expanding the emirate. In 1341, the Byzantine Emperor Andronicus III died and left an 8-year-old successor on the throne. The following civil war created a golden opportunity for the Ottomans to march further into the declining empire and inflict some irreparable damage. The fall of the empire would take another hundred years of power struggles, but there was no way to restore it to its former glory. A six-year-long civil war broke out on the Balkans, and since peace reigned in Orhan's lands, he chose to head further west attempting to create an Ottoman road to Europe.

The Byzantine Grand Domestic John VI Kantakouzenos, who was also the young emperor's custodian and acting as regent, recognized Orhan's potential and formed an alliance with the Ottoman chief. He gave his daughter Theodora in marriage and then used Orhan's help to usurp the throne and become Emperor of Byzantine in 1347. In exchange, Orhan gained the right to plunder Thrace and he started raiding the area regularly through the peninsula of Gallipoli. His oldest son Suleyman took charge of the plundering as Orhan himself was growing older and weaker. The raiding was fruitful and the Ottomans gained both land and riches, while the Byzantine emperor let them. This attracted thousands of uprooted Turkmen to head west and join in Suleyman's expeditions. The emperor of Byzantine had not intended for the Ottomans to actually take possession of Thrace, but that was, of course, inevitable. After Suleyman made Gallipoli into a permanent base for his raiding parties across present-day Bulgaria it didn't take long until John VI was more or less forced to sign over the lands to Orhan's family, a very prestigious win. Constantinople was now surrounded by Ottoman territory, albeit still under Byzantine rule.

It was by the end of Orhan's life that his oldest son died in an accident, which took a toll on Orhan's spirit. He withdrew from power and his last years were spent living quietly in Bursa. Before he died, his youngest son whom he had with Theodora, Sehzade Halil, was kidnapped by pirates along the Aegean coast. It is unclear if they knew who they were kidnapping but when realizing, they took refuge in a Byzantine fortress in Phocaea. After finding this out, Orhan appealed to the co-emperor Andronikos IV to rescue his son and promised in return to call off debts and withdraw his support for the Kantakouzenos family. Andronikus agreed and laid siege to Phocaea, which ended in Orhan paying 30,000 ducats as a ransom for his son. Halil was released in 1359 and it was decided he would marry another Byzantine princess to strengthen the ties between the two dynasties. The imperial family hoped to see Halil as the rightful heir to the beylik since the older brother Suleyman had died.

Their expectations would soon turn into disappointment when Murad was appointed successor to the throne and not the teenager born by Theodora. Murad took over the title and started ruling the emirate after Orhan's death. Orhan was the longest living and ruling chief of all the Ottoman leaders and died in 1362 at the age of 80. Shortly after Orhan's death Murad even had his half-brother executed accused of challenging Murad for the throne. The 16-year-old had already gotten married and produced two young boys who were now left fatherless. This was perhaps the start of brotherly distrust between the heirs of the Ottoman empire. The first Sultans had neglected to formulate an order of succession and it was not until a hundred years later they constituted laws. Hence the throne was up for grabs by any of the sons when a Sultan died, although usually some sort of pre-agreement had been made between the generations. Out of sight from the dead father the avaricious sons almost made it a habit to challenge each other for the throne. After Murad had executed his little brother, many more were to follow his example.

Murad I

Murad transformed the beylik into a Sultanate in 1383 and declared himself Sultan. His right hand, the second lieutenant Lala Sahin Pasa, became the governor of the western province Rumeli while Murad remained in control over Anatolia. At this point, he also instituted an army, referred to as Janissaries, and a recruiting system called Devshirme. This was possible thanks to the reorganization of the military, a seed which was planted by his uncle Alaeddin some 50 years earlier. The Janissaries were an elite infantry loyal only to the Sultan. Their mission was to protect only him and in battles they were always the closest to him, forming a human shield. Originally they consisted of non-Muslim slaves, mainly Christian boys from Byzantium. Jewish boys were not taken as soldiers and Muslims could not, by law, be enslaved. Murad had instituted a tax of one fifth on all the slaves taken in war, and the idea of only taking boys fit for fighting was called Devshirme, or blood tax. The slaves went through a very strict training, first learning to speak Turkish and practicing Ottoman traditions by living with a family chosen by the Sultan. The boys also were forcibly converted to Islam, forbidden from wearing a beard and lived under monastic circumstances in celibacy. They were overseen by eunuchs and trained in special schools, enhancing their personal abilities. The main difference between these and other slaves was that they were being paid for their services. This served as a motivator and kept the soldiers loyal.

The Janissaries were at first a hated institution by the subjugated Christian minorities. Rather than having their sons taken away, it happened that the parents disfigured their children so as to make them weak and unsuitable for Devshirme. But the status of the Janissaries grew. They became men of high learning and an ascetic nature, favored by the Sultan. As they grew in numbers, they also became very influential in the capital and their skills as warriors made them feared far beyond the borders of the empire. The Janissary corps was the first of its kind and a groundbreaking contributor to the success of Ottoman warfare. At the time of Murad's reign, they were fewer and less respected than what they would become at a later stage, though they would prove quite significant when it came to conquering the Balkans.

From the moment Mehmed II succeeded to the Ottoman throne for good in 1451, he took no chance to be vulnerable. For instance, when Murad's widow arrived to congratulate him on his succession, Mehmed received her warmly, but when she returned to her harem she found that her infant son had been drowned in the bath.

That same year, Mehmed moved to secure his borders. He renewed his treaty with Brankovic, leader of Serbia, and created a three-year treaty with Hunyadi, regent of Hungary. He also confirmed a treaty with Venice that his father had made in 1446. All of this would also help further his designs on Constantinople, which the Ottomans had ample reason for coveting. Control of the Bosporus would be extremely advantageous, and control of the Byzantine territory would bring large financial benefits in the form of taxation to the Ottomans. The Ottomans even described the city as their "red apple", an expression for their ultimate aspiration.

Mehmed's attack would be the 13th attempt at conquest against Constantinople, and he intended to do it right. In 1451, he began to build a fortress on the Bosporus at the place where the channel was at its narrowest, opposite Sultan Bayezid's Anadolu Hisar castle. Between the two castles, the Ottomans now had complete control of the Bosporus, which provided them with an ideal base from which to attack Constantinople from the northeast. Emperor Constantine sent embassies to speak with the Ottomans, but they were executed on the spot. Every passing ship was inspected, and when one Venetian ship disobeyed, everyone was killed.

In 1453, Mehmed told his advisors that his empire was not safe as long as Constantinople remained in Christian hands. He began to gather an army in Thrace, and every Ottoman regiment, along with hordes of mercenaries, were recruited; all in all, there were 80,000 regular troops and 20,000 *bashi-bazouks* ("others"), though some historians estimate there were as many as 160,000 troops. Furthermore, the year before, a German engineer called Urban had offered to build the Ottomans a cannon that would blast any walls, so the Ottomans paid for and received the weapon three months later. They then demanded one twice the size and received it in January 1453. It was 27 feet long and 8 inches thick, with a muzzle that was 2.5 feet across, making it capable of shooting a ball some 1,300 pounds a distance of over a mile. 200 men helped the cannon make its journey south to the outside of Constantinople's walls, and their manpower was also needed for smoothing out the road and reinforcing bridges.

Fausto Zorano's painting, *Mehmet II conquering Constantinople*

George Sphrantzes, who was in Constantinople when it fell, wrote about the aftermath: "On the third day after the fall of our city, the Sultan celebrated his victory with a great, joyful triumph. He issued a proclamation: the citizens of all ages who had managed to escape detection were to leave their hiding places throughout the city and come out into the open, as they were remain free and no question would be asked. He further declared the restoration of houses and property to those who had abandoned our city before the siege, if they returned home, they would be treated according to their rank and religion, as if nothing had changed."

Perhaps most notably, after the siege was complete, Mehmed, Tursun Bey, the empire's chief ministers, imams, and the Janissaries rode to the Hagia Sophia. Mehmed picked up a handful of earth and sprinkled it over his turban as he entered as a gesture of humility, and as he approached the altar, he stopped one of the soldiers he saw hacking at the building's marble and informed him that looting did not apply to public buildings. He then commanded the senior imam to ascend to the altar and proclaim the name of Allah. With nothing more than the removal of Christian paraphernalia and their replacement with Muslim pulpits and minarets, the legendary Hagia Sophia became a mosque. The simplicity of the transformation was at once delicate and brutal, as evidenced by the way it's referred to among the Western world and the Turks. In the Christian world, the events are known as "the Fall", but for the Ottomans of history and the Turks of today, it was and remains "the Conquest."

For the Byzantine Empire, losing its beloved capital was the final nail in the coffin, and it didn't take long until the last refuge, Morea on the Peloponnese, was annexed and incorporated by Mehmed. The empire had managed to stay alive for over a thousand years, but after the belligerent rise of the Ottoman Empire, the past century had overwhelmed its rulers. Internal and external conflicts brought the empire to its knees, and the strong unification of the Turkish tribes proved to be a worthy successor of the empire. After the last emperor died without any heirs, all of his nephews were taken into palace service at Mehmed's court. As the two families had many intermarriages and alliances during the years, the boys quickly adapted to life under the Ottoman rule, were converted to Islam, and rose in the ranks of the Sultanate. The youngest nephew later became the grand vizier to Mehmed's son and heir, Bayezid II.

With the takeover of Crimea and Peloponnesus, the Ottomans also came to dominate trade on the Mediterranean and the Black Sea. In the perfect location to be the only gateway between Europe and Asia, the Ottoman Empire became a natural melting pot, which greatly benefited both the rulers and the people living under the empire.

Bayezid II was also notable for his many children as a result of his eight marriages. Not only did he have 8 sons but also 12 daughters, who were married off in politically convenient arrangements with families all around the empire. As Bayezid grew older, his sons became hungry for power and coveted the throne. Even before he was dead, civil war broke out in 1509 between Ahmet and Selim, two of his sons. Ahmet gathered an unexpected army and succeeded in conquering Karamanid, as well as fighting back a Safavid uproar in Asia Minor. Bolstered by the success, he turned toward Constantinople, where his aging father refused to let him in. In his place, Selim found support among the Janissaries and defeated and killed Ahmet in battle. Selim then, more or less, forced his father to abdicate at the age of 62. Bayezid II withdrew to retire in the territory where he'd been born. Just as mysterious and sudden as his father had, Bayezid died on the road, possibly poisoned by the newly acclaimed emperor.

Selim I

Selim started his reign by executing his other brothers and chased his nephew, Ahmet's son, into exile. Selim's rule was short and efficient, but it is generally considered a break in the Pax Ottomana. One cause for Selim's more bellicose persona in comparison to both his father and his future heir was a rising threat in the east - after several decades of relative peace and internal stability, the Sunni Ottoman Muslims discovered a new enemy in the Shiite Persians.

The Safavids

For the Sunni leaders, the Shia Imams always presented an existential threat, but unlike the Umayyads, who justified their rule based upon military victory and the righteousness of the selection of the Caliph Uthman (and his inglorious death), the Abbasids relied upon the Shia argument that their ancestry within the clan of the Prophet Muhammad and direct descent from his uncle Abbas gave them special authority to rule. At the same time, however, it was undeniable that the Shia Imams held the better claim to rule by being descended directly from the Prophet via his favorite daughter Fatima and his beloved, pious, and gallant son-in-law and cousin, Ali. Thus, by arguing for their own legitimacy, the Abbasids also made a strong case for the legitimacy of the Imams. This led to mutual suspicion and the oppression of Shia, especially after the rise of the rival Fatimids.

Once the Fatimid dynasty began to gain power, the scattered Shia communities within the lands of the Abbasid Caliphate came to be viewed as potential fifth columns within their communities. The Sunni-Shia conflicts that characterized this period ended abruptly in 1258, the year the non-Muslim Mongols invaded the Abbasid Caliphate and conquered the city of Baghdad. The previous collapse of the Fatimid Dynasty meant that there was no powerful Shia political force to move into the vacuum, so the two Islamic camps came to a mutual accord in order to unite against an outside force. This invasion shook the Sunnis in particular to the core, as it was the first time that their empire was seriously threatened by a non-Muslim force and the first time that they could not point to the military successes of the Islamic Empire as evidence of God's grace.

The Mongol conqueror Timurlane had made a grant of land in Eastern Anatolia to the Aq Qoyunlu or White Sheep Turks, a confederation of Turkoman nomads, in 1402, but when he died and his empire began to disintegrate, the White Sheep Turks expanded eastward from their seat at Diyar Bakr. By 1470 had established their rule over most of Persia, Mesopotamia, Armenia and Azerbaijan, but their empire would not last long. The Ottomans, desiring to expand eastward, all but destroyed them at the Battle of Otlukbeli in 1473, and when Shah Uzun Hasan died in 1478, the confederation dissolved into civil war between rival Turcoman factions.

Despite having a common enemy, the era of tolerance broke down once again when the Shia regained a political footing. In the far north of the Islamic world, in the city of Ardabil (in today's Iranian Azerbaijan) near the Caspian Sea, a semi-secret order of mystical Sufis called the Safaviyya had existed since the late 13th century. The Safaviyya Order grew in prominence throughout the region and slowly morphed from promoting Sufism (a mystical outgrowth of Sunni thought) to Twelver Shi'ism. In the 1400s, the Order gained a militant aspect and began to build a territorial base for itself, and in 1501, Ismai'il, the leader of the Order (which had been an inherited position for centuries) eventually declared himself "Shah." His new empire was Twelver Shia in character, and the resulting dynasty was called the Safavids.

The Safavids went about recreating the territory of the ancient Persian Empire that had been conquered by the early Rashidun Caliphate, and at their height, the Safavids controlled all of today's Iran, Armenia, and Azerbaijan, as well as large areas of Iraq, Afghanistan, Kuwait, Georgia, Turkey, Syria, Pakistan and Turkmenistan. The Safavids forcibly converted the lands under their rule to Twelver Shi'ism, and also promoted – for the first time in centuries – Persian pride and identity. After centuries of Arab political dominance, the Persians enthusiastically embraced the new identity and, after a time, were willing to fuse their ethnicity with the Shia religion.

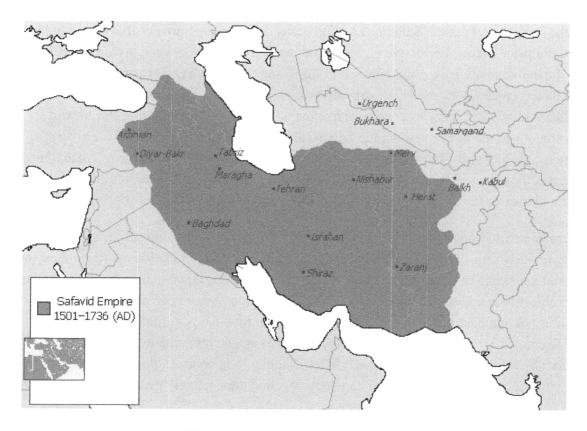

The extent of the Safavid Empire

Much has been made of the brutality of the Safavid conversion of the Persians and the savagery of the conflicts in general, especially amongst Sunni fundamentalist authors who use the term "Safavid" as an insult to describe any pro-Shia Iranian force. It appears that the Safavids sought to convert Persia for several reasons, not only out of a true religious fervor dating back to their days as a secret religious brotherhood but also in order to heighten the differences between their Empire and the Ottomans and prevent fifth column loyalists to the Ottoman Caliphs from undermining their empire. It is important to note that while the Ottomans did not need to convert their population to Sunnism, they used religion just as cynically and showed just as little mercy towards the Shia in their lands as the Safavids did to the Sunni. Moreover, while some states (like the Fatimids) demonstrated a great tolerance within their empires, this was an age of relatively unmitigated brutality and intolerance on the part of all sides.

Regardless of how merciless each side was in comparison to the other, the rise of these two Empires drew an even firmer line between the Sunnis and the Shias, and they provided fresh atrocities for both sides to cite. It also served to catapult Twelver Shi'ism from the political margins to the forefront of the Shia world and, crucially, permanently associated Shi'ism with Iran and the Persians.[12]

---

12 *Islam: Faith, Culture, History* (2002). By Paul Lunde. DK Publishing. Pp 68-73

At the same time, both the Safavids and Ottomans shared characteristics that contributed to their dominance in their respective regions. Both were founded by a warrior caste (Turkic in the case of the Ottomans, Turkic and Kurdish in Iran), and tribal leaders were granted land in return for military service. Both were ethnically diverse empires unified by a common religion, but significant religious minorities continued to exist in both. In both dominions, the apex of government was the monarch, with the Sultan ruling the Ottoman Empire and the Shah governing the Safavids. They were absolute rulers who governed in the name of Allah, though in both cases they were restricted by Islamic law as interpreted by the *Ulema*, the college of Muslim clerics and scholars. In both empires, culture and learning flourished.

There were also important differences. Under the Sultans, non-Muslim subjects were governed by the *millet* system. This regime allowed Christian and Jewish populations to retain their own laws and a measure of religious freedom. They were, however, taxed higher than Muslims and were subject to *devsirme*, the practice of taking young boys to be raised as Muslims and trained in military or administrative service. This meant that in time the government and military became ethnically diverse rather than exclusively Turkish, so referring to the Ottoman Empire as a "Turkish" empire is actually somewhat of a misnomer.[13] In contrast, the Safavid elite were more ethnically homogenous and Persian-speaking, and they actively persecuted non-Muslims.[14]

Of course, the fundamental difference that brought the two sides into open conflict concerned religion. Iran had been predominantly Sunni before the reign of Shah Ismail I. Claiming to rule in the place of the hidden Mahdi and to be the descendant and living embodiment of the Prophet Mohammed,[15] he set about fanatically persecuting the Sunni as heretics and vowed to exterminate the abomination from the face of the Earth.[16] He ordered the destruction of Sunni mosques, the ritual cursing of the first three Sunni caliphs, the massacres of Sunni clerics who refused to convert, and the desecration of the graves of prominent Sunnis. Such fanatical hatred in so young a monarch must have been seen as both provocative and troubling to the Ottoman Sultans, who regarded themselves as the defenders of Sunni Islam. Though there was still a Sunni caliph reigning in Egypt, they had claimed the moral authority of the caliphate since Sultan Murad I.

What was immediately concerning to Sultan Bayezid II was the presence of Shia adherents in the provinces of Ottoman Anatolia, actively encouraged by the young Shah. To them, the Sunni regime was unholy and irreconcilable, and the Sultan feared the fanatical terrorism that characterized the new Iranian Safavid regime exported into his own lands. Indeed, such trepidations were not unfounded, because even before Ismail proclaimed himself Shah, a Shia whirling dervish had attempted to assassinate Bayezid II in 1492.

---

[13] Soucek, Svat (2015). *Ottoman Maritime Wars, 1416–1700*. Istanbul: The Isis Press. p. 8.

[14] Streusand, Douglas (2010) E. *Islamic Gunpowder Empires: Ottomans, Safavids, and Mughals*. Boulder, CO: Westview, p. 165–166.

[15] "Esmaʿil i Ṣafawi" *Encyclopedia Iranica*, http://www.iranicaonline.org/articles/esmail-i-safawi.

[16] Daniel W. Brown (2004), *A new introduction to Islam*, Malden, MA: Blackwell Pub. p.191.

Ismail I

Upon the Shah's accession, Turcomen converted to Shia and migrated from Anatolia to Iran in such numbers that the borders were depopulated.[17] The Safavid brand of Islam greatly appealed to the recently conquered and alienated populations of Anatolia. Those Shia militants, the *Qizilbash*, who remained in Anatolia were considered threats to the state, and as early as 1502 Bayezid moved great numbers of them to Greece, where they were not considered as much of a danger.

In 1511, the Sahkulu Rebellion occurred in central and southern Anatolia and even had supporters in Rumelia, the European part of the Ottoman Empire.[18] It originated with the Turkoman tribes in the Taurus Mountains and rapidly spread to groups disaffected by the Ottoman regime. The cause of the revolt was not entirely religious - recent famines and plague, to which the authorities in Constantinople seemed indifferent, pushed them to armed rebellion. The Anatolian Turkoman tribesmen already had a longstanding grievance against the Ottomans over their attempts to bring them under direct control. Many may have genuinely believed Ismail to be a divine figure, but the Safavid form of government, still based on Turkic tribalism, must have appealed to them even more.

[17] Nazeer Ahmed, "The Battle of Chaldiran", *History of Islam: An Encyclopedia of Islamic History*, https://historyofislam.com/contents/the-land-empires-of-asia/the-battle-of-chaldiran/.

[18] Caroline Finkel, *Osman's Dream: The story of the Ottoman Empire 1300–1923*, Hatchette, UK. p.

The revolt was led by Sahkulu of the Turcoman Tekkelu tribe, who seemed to have been genuinely moved by the cause of the Safavids thanks to the influence of Shia missionaries. He was caught up in the same messianic fervor that animated Ismail's followers in Persia. He began his rebellion by sacking the caravan of Prince Korkut, who was moving his court from Antalya to Manisa, an Anatolian city on the Aegean. Following this audacious attack, he devastated the towns of Anatolia and killed its governors.

Sultan Bayezid II sent an army lead by Karagoz Ahmed Pasha, the Governor of Kastamonu, but this force was defeated and Ahmed was executed. The victory greatly enhanced Sakhulu's standing and increased his followers, much to the dismay of Bayezid II, who next sent Prince Ahmed and the Grand Vizier, Hadim Ali Pasha. Bayezid II would have preferred not to empower Ahmed with an army, for his sons were engaged in a contest for his throne, but he had little choice. As it happened, Ahmed failed to engage Sakhulu and allowed him to escape. Hadim Ali pursued him alone and brought him to battle at Cuhukova, in central Anatolia. Both Sakhulu and the Grand Vizier perished, and the opposing forces left the field without deciding anything.

A third army was sent, and this finally dispersed the leaderless *Qizilbash*. Many of its leaders fled to Ismail, who nevertheless executed them for accidentally killing a famous Persian scholar. At the same time, the Shah's disavowal of the rebellion did nothing to ease Bayezid II's continued anxieties for Anatolia. Instead of dealing with rebellious Turcomen harshly, he offered Ismail the hand of friendship, at least superficially. He believed he had good reason to do so, given that the rebellion had almost seized Anatolia from his control. No doubt fearing a second uprising might succeed, Bayezid II addressed Ismail in flattering terms, calling him the successor of Darius and heir to the kingdom of Khay Khosrow, both renowned kings of ancient Persia, and he is said to have counselled moderation to the young sovereign in the manner that a father would a son. Undoubtedly, the young Shah viewed this as an expression of weakness on the part of the Sultan, which also happened to be a view shared by many Ottomans, including Prince Selim. As such, Ismail spurned the advice.

The Sahkulu Rebellion had played into the Ottoman succession crisis. The rebellion might have been crushed decisively if it were not for the ambitions of Bayezid II's son, Prince Ahmed, who instead of confronting Sahkulu attempted to win his own troops over in a plot to overthrow his father with Safavid backing. This they refused to do, and this gave strength to the cause of Prince Selim, another of Bayezid II's sons. It helped Selim's cause that Halim Ahmed, the slain Grand Vizier, had been Prince Ahmed's most powerful supporter. Selim had fled to the Crimea in August 1511 after raising an army against his father, but his brother's attempted treason now brought him closer to the throne. Ahmed failed to seize the capital, Constantinople, through lack of support from the military, but Bayezid II was a spent force and he knew it.

The Sultan had little energy for war and longed to be relieved of the burden of government,[19]

---

[19] Christopher Marciewicz (2019), *The Crisis of Kingship in Late Medieval Islam*, Cambridge University Press

so he recalled Selim from exile even though he knew it would mean his abdication. Selim was triumphantly girded with the Sword of Osman on April 24, 1512, and the ex-Sultan was retired to Thrace, where he died soon after.[20] He was almost certainly poisoned by the new Sultan. It would be remarkable, given the savage contests and bloody deeds that permeated the Ottoman succession, if Bayezid II did not anticipate his fate.

Whatever the case, Selim marched into Anatolia and defeated and executed Ahmed. He also executed his remaining brother and his nephews, with the exception of Prince Murad (1495–1515), who joined Safavid-backed Shia forces in Anatolia led by the Turcoman Nur-Ali Khalifa.

The Leaders and Their Armies

In 1513, Selim learned that Ismail planned to conquer Anatolia and install Murad as its *bey* (governor).[21] The Sultan knew he had to act swiftly, so he secured a fatwa from the *Ulema* branding the Shia as heretics. War against fellow Muslims was forbidden, but jihad against the heretic and unbeliever was a sacred duty. He now possessed the legal authority to enact savage measures, including the execution of around 40,000 *Qizilbash*.

Encouraged by the defeat of a Safavid army at the hands of the Uzbeks in Armenia in 1512, Selim was resolved to invade Iran and strike at the source of the Anatolian rebellion. By the summer of 1514, he determined his men were ready, so he set off through Anatolia with his army.

Before the conflict began, Selim and Ismail exchanged letters, written in florid style as was the custom, making appeals to the Qu'ran and including barbed poetry. Persian was the language of poetry, which was considered the *lingua franca* of the Middle East.

The Sultan wrote to the Shah:

> "When I draw my keen-edged weapon from its sheath,
>
> Then shall I raise up doomsday on the earth;
>
> Then shall I roast the hearts of lion-hearted men,
>
> And toast the morning with a goblet of their blood.
>
> My crow-fletched shaft will fix the eagle in his flight;

p.117.

[20] H. Erdem Cipa (2017), *The Making of Selim: Succession, Legitimacy and Memory in the Early Modern Ottoman World*, Indiana University Press p.15.

[21] Faroqhi, Suraiya; Fleet, Kate, eds. (2012). *The Cambridge History of Turkey (Vol. 2): The Ottoman Empire as World Power, 1453–1603*. Cambridge: Cambridge University Press. pp. 1–723.

And my bare blade will shake the orb of day.

Ask of the sun about the dazzle of my rein;

Inquire of Mars about the brilliance of my arms.

Although you wear a Sufi crown, I bear a trenchant sword,

And he who holds the sword will soon possess the crown.

O Mighty Fortune, pray grant this my single wish:

Please let me take both crown and power from the foe."[22]

In response to these bold words, Ismail wrote in even loftier tones, filled with majesty and self-assurance. He reminded Selim that the Ottomans had been defeated by the Timurids in 1402, and that Anatolia had risen in sedition at the time. The same would happen again, as "most of the inhabitants of the land of Rum [Anatolia] are followers of our forefathers..." He declared that he was not moved by Selim's provocations, which he attributed to the Sultan's "opium-clouded" secretaries. Ismail ended his missive with this threat:

"Bitter experience has taught that in this world of trial

He who falls upon the house of 'Ali always falls."[23]

As the messages amply demonstrate, neither ruler had any intention of seeking a compromise to avoid war. For both, war was a necessity, and their communications were dictated purely by diplomatic courtesy and the Islamic rules of warfare. Selim believed his very throne was at stake, and Ismail saw the opportunity to remove a potentially powerful enemy.

For the Sultan, the campaign was beset with difficulties from the beginning. The march through Asia Minor, still seething with rebellion, was arduous, and supplies were limited. Furthermore, the Anatolian summer was punishing. He dared not recruit any of the Turcomen lest they turn on him, but he also could not guarantee that the troops he had would not do so.

In the eastern part of Anatolia, Ismail's army was outnumbered and at a disadvantage, so the Persians refused to give battle, especially since Selim's allies, the Shaybanids of central Asia, were attacking the eastern borders. Ismail pulled back into Armenia, laying the countryside to waste as he did so in order to deprive the Ottoman army of supplies. He must have also known that the soldiers in Selim's camp were expressing misgivings about having to fight fellow Muslims and were on the verge of mutiny. The Janissaries, the Sultan's elite slave-soldiers, even

---

[22] https://www.shiachat.com/forum/topic/235020699-the-poetry-of-Shah-ismail-i/
[23] Ibid.

fired upon Selim's tent as they camped at Lake Van in Armenia. The Shah may have believed that the army would turn on the Sultan or at least that some of his troops would return home.

Ironically, the Ottoman army might have turned on its leader and headed back had it not been for the sighting of Ismail and the Safavid army about 22 miles northeast of Lake Van. The army, galvanized by the prospect of imminent battle, broke camp under their Sultan and marched off to confront the Safavid forces.

For Selim, the stakes were as high as they could be. If he failed to defeat the Shah, Anatolia would most likely turn against the Ottomans and place itself under the protection of the Safavids. Even if he survived the battle, he could not rule an empire without Anatolia, and Rumelia would be more vulnerable to attack from the Christian Europeans. The capital of the Ottoman Empire, Constantinople, was in Europe, as was its main source of military and economic strength, but its origins and spiritual heart lay in the Anatolian highlands, as did its trade routes to Asia. The very survival of the empire therefore depended upon an Ottoman victory. Selim would have also been aware that the Christian powers of central Europe and the Mediterranean, including much of Italy and the Vatican, Hungary, Poland, and Spain all cast their eyes hopefully to Persia. If the Safavids broke Ottoman power in Anatolia, then these powers might combine to do so in Europe.

Selim I, known to history as The Grim or The Resolute, was born in 1470 to Bayezid II and his consort Gulbahar Hatun, the daughter of an Anatolian prince. When Sultan Mehmed II died in 1481 and Bayezid II succeeded him, Selim became, at the age of 11, one of eight rival heirs to the Ottoman throne. Succession in the Ottoman state was not by primogeniture as in most Western monarchies; instead, the sons of the sovereign vied with each other for the throne, and the losers were usually strangled by the new Sultan. The sons then spent their lives positioning themselves for the succession, if not out of ambition, then for their very survival. This ruthlessness was theoretically supposed to ensure that the most able son succeeded. Moreover, it maintained stability by removing potential usurpers.

The royal princes were habitually made governors of provinces, which was considered an important part of their education. The location of the province could be very important, for a prince residing closest to Constantinople had the best chance of claiming the throne when the Sultan died. Thus, appointments near the capital were regarded as evidence of royal favour.

Selim was made *Sanjak-bey* (Governor) of Trebizond (Trabzon) on the Black Sea coast, over 1600 miles east of the capital, in 1495, accompanied by his mother, who was naturally solicitous to ensure that her son became the next Sultan. This was not a good omen for an Ottoman prince, and from his youth Selim must have realized that he had to be strong and ruthless to survive.

By the time of the Sakhulu Rebellion, only three prince-governors survived: Ahmed, Korkut and Selim. Ahmed, the eldest, had been made Governor of Amasya in north-central Anatolia, only 420 miles from Constantinople, whereas Korkut resided at Saruhan (Manisa), a little over

250 miles south of the capital in southwestern Anatolia. Ahmed was clearly Bayezid II's favorite, whereas Selim seemed to have no advantage whatsoever and would almost certainly be executed by his brother if he replaced his father. It is unsurprising then that he attempted to seize the throne while his father was still alive.

Selim had an energetic and intense personality. He was choleric and compulsive, with little tolerance for failure. His physical stature, tall with broad shoulders, matched his bellicose and imposing character. He had grand plans for the Ottoman state and is known to have executed seven of his Grand Viziers when they could not meet his exacting standards. A popular curse in the Ottoman Empire was, "May you be Sultan Selim's Grand Vizier!"[24]

The first task on Selim's agenda was the eradication of the Shiite threat. His father had been prepared to tolerate it to some extent, and he had even reached out to the Ismailites, but Bayezid II ultimately failed to contain the movement. Selim believed this to have been his father's greatest mistake and weakness. Pus simply, Selim would spill blood where Bayezid II would not.

When he set off with his army in the summer of 1514, Selim had not yet reached his 44th birthday, so he was still in his prime and full of vigour. He was accompanied by Hashan Pasha, who commanded the left flank at Chaldiran, and Hadim Sinan Pasha, the *Beylerbey* (Governor-general) of all of Anatolia, who led the right flank. Hadim Sinan Pasha was a Bosnian *Devsirme* and would become Grand Vizier in 1516. Indeed, he was one of the few officers to fittingly (at least in Selim's eyes) share the Sultan's vision for the empire, and his death at the Battle of Ridaniya in Egypt in 1517 was genuinely mourned.[25]

Estimates of the size of the Ottoman army vary from 60,000-100,000,[26][27] reflecting the frustrating lack of details kept in medieval and early modern times, but it is known the Ottoman military was one of the finest and best organized in the world. It was composed of two elements: the *Kapiculu*, troops of the imperial household, and the *Eyalet*, or provincial musters. The *Kapiculu Ocagi*, literally "Slaves of the Porte," were slaves and were comprised of the *Yeniceri* and the *Kapiculu Suvarileri*.

The *Yeniceri* (new soldiers) or Janissaries were the empire's elite infantry corps. They were mostly sons of Christian families taken at an early age and raised in the Islamic faith who became full-time professional soldiers, expertly educated not only in warfare but in religion and culture as well. Indeed, they were amongst the most educated in the Ottoman Empire, placed in positions of authority in both the government and military, and it was not at all unusual that the Sultan chose his Grand Viziers from the ranks of the Janissaries. They considered themselves the

[24] Mike Dash (2012), "The Ottoman Empire's Life-or-Death Race", *Smithsonian.com*
https://www.smithsonianmag.com/history/the-ottoman-empires-life-or-death-race-164064882/.
[25] Prof. Yaşar Yüce-Prof (1991). Ali Sevim: *Türkiye tarihi Cilt II*, AKDTYKTTK Yayınları, İstanbul, pp. 248–249
[26] Keegan & Wheatcroft (1996), *Who's Who in Military History*, Routledge p. 268.
[27] *Encyclopedia of the Ottoman Empire* (2009), ed. Gábor Ágoston, Bruce Alan Masters, page 286.

elite defenders of Islam and were devoted to the Sultan, though rebellions were not unheard of. In order to keep their loyalty, the Janissaries were forbidden to marry or trade and thus establish power bases outside of the imperial household.

Janissaries trained according to a strict discipline, in monastery-like institutions known as *acemi oglan.* They "graduated" at the age of 24 or 25, when they gained the right to wear the distinctive white headdress known as the bork. They were salaried, unlike most other military units of the time, and wore distinctive uniforms and lived in barracks.

Türkei.

Janitscharen.
16. u. 17. Jahrhundert.

Depictions of Janissaries

An 18th century depiction of the commander of the Janissaries

The Janissary Corps was governed by an *Agha*, chosen by the Sultan and one who was not necessarily a Janissary himself. The primary Janissary unit was the *orta*, commanded by a *corbaci*. An appropriate Western equivalent might be a colonel.

The ortas made up three sub-corps: the Sultan's bodyguard (*boluk*), the border garrisons (*cemaat*), and the regulars (*sekban*). Promotion through the ranks was by seniority rather than merit alone, and a soldier could only rise within his own orta. It was only when he assumed the position of *corbaci* that he might be transferred to command another battalion.

The Janissaries were light infantrymen, unarmored and expert in the bow and melee combat, during which they used axes and sabers. The *yatagan*, a short, dagger-like saber, became a signature Janissary weapon.

By the time of the Battle of Chaldiran, the Janissaries had also become expert in the use of firearms. The musket was first introduced to the Ottoman army towards the end of the 15th century, about 50 years before it was adopted by Europeans.[28] Janissaries were also expert

---

[28] Ayalon, David (2013). *Gunpowder and Firearms in the Mamluk Kingdom: A Challenge to Medieval Society*

sappers, miners and engineers, though they were yet to come to prominence. Selim's son and successor, Suleiman I the Magnificent (r. 1520–1566), would employ them during the famous Siege of Vienna in 1529.

Contrary to prevailing belief, the Janissaries made up only a small proportion of the Ottoman army. Toward the end of the 15th century, there were close to 8,000 in the whole of the empire.[29] Their number never exceeded 10% of the army,[30] and the contingent at Chaldiran numbered no more than 12,000.

The *Kapiculu Suvarileri* was a corps of elite slave-cavalry, representing the mounted counterpart of the Janissary corps. It was composed of six divisions and was probably founded by Sultan Murad I (r. 1362–1389).[31] Originally composed of the sons of the nobility, it was later reformed to include *devsirme* and other classes based on merit and loyalty to the Sultan. In the mid-15th century, its strength was around 8,000.[32]

The *Suvarileri* were elite heavy cavalry and wore chain or plate mail, bore a round shield and wielded swords, bows, maces, axes and lances. They did not, however, use firearms until the last quarter of the 16th century. They differed from their Janissary counterparts in that they were not necessarily recruited directly from the *devsirme*. Janissaries were often recruited, and free peasants might be also. However, if a freeman was inducted into the household cavalry, he automatically lost his free status.

The *Suvarileri* were tasked with guarding the person of the Sultan and the imperial court, though they were often employed in battle as reinforcements. As the Sultan's bodyguards, they would undoubtedly have been present at Chaldiran.

The bulk of Selim's army was composed of the *Elayet* (provincial) musters, both infantry and cavalry. The *Yaya* (walkers) were volunteer light infantry, recruited largely from peasant communities. Unlike the Janissaries, they were not full-time soldiers and were obliged to procure their own weapons. They usually worked in their fields in peacetime and, at the time of Chaldiran, were exempted from taxation in return for military service. Originally, they were salaried, but they proved unreliable due to their lack of military training and discipline. As

---

[29] Ágoston, Gábor (2014). "Firearms and Military Adaptation: The Ottomans and the European Military Revolution, 1450–1800". *Journal of World History*. 25: 113.

[30] Nicolle, David (1995). *The Janissaries*. London: Osprey Publishing, pp. 9–10.

[31] Mesut Uyar, Edward J. Erickson (2009), *A Military History of the Ottomans: From Osman to Atatürk*, ABC-CLIO p.44.

[32] Ibid, p. 45.

combat troops they had little value and they were sometimes used as bait to draw enemy units into combat. At the time of the Battle of Chaldiran, the *yaya* were auxiliary troops, employed in transport, baggage trains and other duties, though they could of course be sent into combat when necessity demanded it.

In the late 14th century, the combat role of the *yaya* was replaced by the *azap* (bachelor). These were peasant youths (originally unmarried), and like the *yaya* before them, they were volunteers. Unlike the later *yaya*, they were paid during wartime. At the time of the Battle of Chaldiran, only Anatolian Turks could serve in the ranks of the *azap* and they were not obliged to a fixed term. Like the *yaya*, they were expected to provide their own weapons, usually composite bows, swords and sometimes pole weapons such as halberds.

The bulk of the cavalry, and indeed the bulk of the army in this period, was made up of *timariots*, aristocratic holders of *timars* or grants of taxable land who were obliged to provide battle-ready cavalry equipped and maintained at their own expense. It was from the *timars* that the famous *sipahi* were drawn. The name comes from the Persian for "warrior." Unlike knights in medieval Europe, they did not own their land, which belonged to the Sultan, but had the right to govern and tax its inhabitants, as well as the obligation to protect them.

Timar sipahis were freeborn and Muslim. In battle they marched under the banner of their provincial governor, and there was a distinction between Rumelian (European) and Anatolian *sipahi*. The latter fought principally as horse archers while the former were more heavily armored and used lances and javelins, resembling the cataphracts of the Byzantine Empire and 7th century Persia.

The light Ottoman cavalry were known as *akinci* (raiders). They were descendants of the first Ottoman cavalry of the 14th century, the *ghazi*, and lived along the borders of the Ottoman Empire. They lived by plundering their neighbours. They did not possess *timars*, nor were they salaried - they fought solely for the spoils of war. Like the Anatolian *sipahi*, they were skilled horse archers but more lightly equipped, meaning they could fire on advancing troops while riding and then withdraw before them, out of range and still firing. This produced a demoralizing effect which contributed greatly to the success of the heavier *sipahi*. The *akinci* were also used as scout troops on account of their swiftness and dexterity.

The Ottoman Artillery Corps (*Topcu Ocagi*) was one of the finest in the world at the time and gave the army a distinct advantage over most enemy forces. The Ottoman military was one of the first in the world to systematically and effectively deploy cannon and other gunpowder artillery in battle, at least from the mid-15th century and probably earlier.[33] The technology was borrowed from the West, but it was not long before the Ottomans made the technology their own. Huge bronze cannons were used to bring down the walls of Constantinople in 1453, and some of the

---

[33] David Nicolle (1983) *Armies of the Ottoman Turks 1300–1774,,* Angus McBride p.18

bombards used in that siege were so large that it took 200 men and 60 oxen to move one. They weighed 17 tonnes (19 tons) and could only fire 7 times a day. Selim may have had as many as 200 cannons[34] and 100 mortars at Chaldiran.[35]

Shah Ismail I was still just 27 when the Battle of Chaldiran was fought, but he had known violence and unrest since the death of his father, Shaykh Haydar, in 1488. His mother was Halim Begum, the daughter of Uzun Hasan and a descendant of John IV (r. 1429–1455), Greek Emperor of Trebizond (Turkish Trabzon). Haydar was head of the Safavid Order before him and had galvanized its adherents into a political force. This was at a time when the regime of the White Sheep Turks was collapsing from internal division. Haydar perished in a battle with the Turks in what is now Dagestan.

The infant Ismail was thereupon taken to live in hiding in Gilan in north-western Persia. His older brother Ali Marza was in the meantime proclaimed head of the order and PadiShah ("Great King" or "Emperor"), the title used by the rulers of Persia before the Muslim conquest. The Turks arrested him, but he escaped, only to be used by a claimant to the Persian throne for his own ends. He was eventually killed by the Turks in 1494, but not before appointing Ismail his successor.

As a boy, Ismail thus grew up believing that his family was a sacred one that had a God-given mission. His father and his brother were martyrs for the true religion and considered the rightful representatives of the Prophet Mohammed and God's vice-regents in the temporal world. They were considered "the living emanation of the godhead, the Shadow of God upon earth."[36] One could only imagine the sense of entitlement and responsibility that molded the mind of the 6-year-old boy after Ali Marza died. Ismail was considered the representative of the last imam, the Mahdi who was living in secret, hidden by Allah, who would return at the end of time to complete the victory of Islam. Some followers went even further and declared Ismail to be the very image of God himself.[37] It is easy to see the attraction of such a leader, given that obedience to him promised security and unity in a nation stricken by internal and external conflict. One may also appreciate the alarm in foreign rulers such as Selim, who found himself facing a man who could command armies with the obedience of faith, convinced of his God-given right to rule the world.

One Turkish devotee, the renowned poet Sultan Abdal, penned a poem of adulation in Ismail's honor:

"He makes a march against Urum

---

[34] Ágoston, Gábor (2014). "Firearms and Military Adaptation: The Ottomans and the European Military Revolution, 1450–1800". *Journal of World History*. **25**: 110.

[35] Savory, Roger (2007). *Iran Under the Safavids*. Cambridge: Cambridge University Press, p.42.

[36] Ibid, p. 33.

[37] Ibid.

The Imam of Ali's descent is coming
I bow down and kissed his Hand
The Imam of Ali's descent is coming

"He fills the cups step by step
In his stable only noble Arab horses
His ancestry, he is the son of the Shah
The Imam of Ali's descent is coming

"The fields are marked step by step
His rival makes his heart aching
Red-green is the young warrior dressed
The Imam of Ali's descent is coming

"He lets him seen often on the field
No one knows the secret of the saviour
Shah of the world goodman Haydar's grandson
The Imam of Ali's descent is coming

"Pir Sultan Abdal, I am, if i could see this
Submit myself, if I could wipe my face at him
From ere he is the leader of the 12 Imams
The Imam of Ali's descent is coming."[38]

When Ismail reached the age of 12, about the time Muslim boys are considered adults, he came out of hiding and returned to the family lands in Ardabil, Azerbaijan, where he gained the support of the tribes there. He also drew support from the Turcomen of Eastern Anatolia, many of whom were disillusioned with their Ottoman overlords. It is from these Turkish tribes that the formidable *Qizilbash* arose, and with their help he challenged the ineffectual last White Sheep ruler, Murad ibn Yaq'ub.

The young Grand Master's meteoric rise to power must have convinced him that the power of God did indeed reside within him, especially when he defeated an army four times the size of his own at the Battle of Sarur in 1501. Indeed, the image he held of himself is reflected in much of his poetry, which includes the following:

"Today I have come to the world as a Master. Know truly that I am Haydar's son.
I am Fereydun, Khosrow, Jamshid, and Zahak. I am Zal's son (Rostam) and
Alexander.
The mystery of I am the truth is hidden in this my heart. I am the Absolute Truth

and what I say is Truth.
I belong to the religion of the 'Adherent of the Ali' and on the Shah's path I am a
guide to everyone who says: 'I am a Muslim.' My sign is the 'Crown of Happiness'.
I am the signet-ring on Sulayman's finger. Muhammad is made of light, Ali of
Mystery.
I am a pearl in the sea of Absolute Reality.'[39]

By way of contrast, Selim I, also an accomplished poet, as many Middle Eastern potentates
were, wrote of himself in less mystical and more martial tones:

> "From Istambol's throne a mighty host to Iran guided I;
> Sunken deep in blood of shame I made the Golden Heads to lie.
> Glad the Slave, my resolution, lord of Egypt's realm became:
> Thus I raised my royal banner e'en as the Nine Heavens high.
> From the kingdom fair of Iraq to Hijaz these tidings sped,
> When I played the harp of Heavenly Aid at feast of victory.
> Through my saber Transoxania drowned was in a sea of blood;
> Emptied I of kohl of Isfahan the adversary's eye.
> Flowed adown a River Amu from each foeman's every hair---
> Rolled the sweat of terror's fever---if I happed him to espy.
> Bishop-mated was the King of India by my Queenly troops,
> When I played the Chess of empire on the Board of sovreignty.
> O Selimi, in thy name was struck the coinage of the world,
> When in crucible of Love Divine, like gold, that melted I."[40]

The new Shah almost immediately proclaimed Twelver Shia to be the new state religion, and
Ismail's youthful idealism and intolerance is exhibited in the brutality by which he converted
Persia. The idealist is often ruthless, and destructively so, if extreme youth is matched with a
sense of God-ordained purpose. It is probable that much of the savage persecution of Sunni
Muslims was conducted by those acting in his name, but without his explicit consent or
knowledge. Nonetheless, there must have been a degree to which he knew what was happening
and blessed the actions of his ministers.

In appearance, Ismail was handsome and physically impressive. An Italian visitor to the
Safavid court wrote of him, "This Sophi [Safavid] is fair, handsome, and very pleasing; not very
tall, but of a light and well-framed figure; rather stout than slight, with broad shoulders. His hair
is reddish; he only wears moustachios [that is, he does not wear a beard], and uses his left hand
instead of his right. He is as brave as a game cock, and stronger than any of his lords; in the

---

[39] Newman, Andrew J. (2008). *Safavid Iran: Rebirth of a Persian Empire*. I.B.Tauris, p.13.
[40] "Ottoman Turks' Poetry", *Ottoman Souvenir*
https://www.ottomansouvenir.com/General/Turkish_Poetry.htm#Gazel5.

archery contests, out of the ten apples that are knocked down, he knocks down seven."[41]

In his physical prowess, drive, natural ability and awareness of his God-given right to rule, Ismail was much like his adversary Selim. Both came to their thrones through dynastic violence, though in the case of Selim, he had been the instigator as well as the recipient of such violence.

In the Chaldiran campaign, Ismail was accompanied by Abd al-Baqi Yazdi, an important figure in the nascent Safavid state. Little is known of him, but he came from Yazd in central Iran and was the leader of another Sufi order, the Nematollahi, which threw in its lot with the Safavids. He was the *Vakil*, the Shah's regent, in whom the offices of commander-in-chief, spiritual overseer and chief executive were combined, unlike in the Ottoman Empire where the institutions of Grand Vizier and Ulema were separated. Hossein Beg Laleh Shamlu, who also held a command with Ismail, had also been Vakil but was replaced by Abd al-Baqi. He was a *Qizilbash* and the leader of the Turcoman Shamlu clan, one of the first to support the young Shah in his rise to power and one of the closest to the throne. Durmish Khan Shamlu was Beg Laleh's son and the governor of Isfahan. He was to play a fateful role during the battle.

Two other commanding officers at Chaldiran were of particular significance: Mohammed Khan Ustajlu and Nur-Ali Khalifa. Both were Turcomen who played crucial roles in the Safavid conquest of Iran, and both officers were experts in Ottoman warfare. They would offer important advice to Ismail on the course of the battle, and his failure to follow that advice would cost him dearly.

The Safavid army consisted almost entirely of mounted archers, the most important of which were the *Qizilbash*, the militarized followers of the Safavid Order. They traced their origins to Ismail's father, Shayk Hadar, who organized his followers into an elite militia. As with the Ottoman army, estimates of the number of *Qizilbash* at Chaldiran vary from as few as 40,000[42] to as many as 80,000.[43] These were mostly of Turkic origin, recruited from Azerbaijan, Kurdistan, and Anatolia. They derived their name, "red-headed," from their crimson headwear and were fanatically devoted to the head of the Safavi Order, whom they regarded as representative of God. They considered themselves alone worthy of protecting the Shah and the holy Shia state, and they looked down upon the Iranian population, which they referred to derisively as *Tajik* ("non-Turks").[44] They addressed Ismail as *PadiShah – i – Qizilbash* ("Emperor of the *Qizilbash*"), completely ignoring all other tribal groups.

This fanatical devotion certainly had its advantages, but also a serious disadvantage in that it prevented Ismail from drawing other factions into his base of power to augment his army. This last problem was evident at Chaldiran, where the Safavids had no gunpowder weapons or

[41] "ESMĀʿĪL I ṢAFAWĪ – Encyclopaedia Iranica". *iranicaonline.org*.
[42] Savory, p. 41.
[43] *Encyclopedia of the Ottoman Empire* (2009), ed. Gábor Ágoston, Bruce Alan Masters, p. 286.
[44] Savory, p. 42.

artillery of any sort. The *Qizilbash* commanders frowned upon them, considering them dishonorable and contemptuous,[45] and they preferred to rely on traditional weapons such as swords, spears, axes, maces and the composite bow. These problems would be overcome, though the Safavids, believing themselves to be guided by God, could not yet see them.

A special unit of the *Qizilbash* is worthy of note. This was *Qurchi* (archer), which functioned as the personal guard of the Shah and his palaces, making them the Safavid equivalent of the Ottoman Suvarileri. Like the latter, they were individually recruited and salaried, unlike the tribal *Qizilbash*, and might be granted land as well. The commander of the *Qurchi* was known as the *Qurch-bashi*. There were about 3,000 of these royal soldiers at Chaldiran.[46] Ismail's successors would increase their size, because their dependence upon the person of the Shah made them more reliable than the conservative and fanatical *Qizilbash*. For this reason, *Qurchi* were assigned as garrison troops. Ismail's successors even made them provincial governors, and the *Qurchi-bashi* became one of the most powerful officers of the state. The *Qurchi* were not slave-soldiers (*gholam*) as the Janissaries and Suvarileri were, but later on in the 16th century, a *gholam* corps was created out of Georgian, Circassian, and Armenian slaves.

The Battle of Chaldiran

Selim was relieved that he could at least bring the Shah to battle. As he marched into Eastern Anatolia, the Safavids had consistently withdrawn east, and with the towns evacuated of their troops and governors, Selim's army simply took possession of them. The surrender of the Kurdish city of Diyarbarkir, one of the largest citadels of the region and the spiritual home of the Anatolian *Qizilbash*, should have been an occasion for rejoicing, but Selim was uneasy, much like Napoleon would be when his army invaded Russia largely unopposed nearly 300 years later. The withdrawing *Qizilbash* had destroyed all resources that the enemy could use, including food supplies, and as the Sultan pressed further into enemy territory, he discovered that he could not replenish his supplies. Furthermore, he risked facing Ismail in autumn or winter, which might mean the Ottomans faced poor conditions with no food and no prospect of a safe retreat.

Ismail and his army were at Khoy, in what is now West Azerbaijan Province in Iran, about 350 miles east of Diyarbarkir. It was a formidable defensive position located in the mountains. Selim would have been forced to fight in difficult and unfamiliar terrain, and it would have been difficult if not impossible to transport artillery. However, Ismail and his *Qizilbash* left the fortress and descended into the plains between Khoy and Urumiah, about 100 miles northwest of the Safavid capital, Tabriz. It is unclear why he made the decision to confront Selim where he did, which just so happened to be a position ideal for artillery. It may be that he changed his mind about risking the fall of Tabriz in order to maintain a defensive advantage, or perhaps he

---

[45] Kaveh Farrock, *Iran at War* 1500–1988, Osprey Publishing p. 25 &31.

[46] Haneda, Masashi (1989). *The Evolution of the Safavid Royal Guard*. Journal of Near Eastern Studies, vol. 22, no. 2/3. P. 67.

believed that God would grant him victory under any circumstances.

Whatever the Shah's motives, he positioned his army on the plain on the early morning of August 23, 1514. Meanwhile, Selim selected a hill and began to position his artillery. At this point, the Sultan was vulnerable, and Ismail might have attacked him before his artillery was ready had he listened to the advice of the two commanders with experience of Ottoman battle tactics, Mohammed Khan Ustajlu and Nur-Ali Khalifa. An attack at this point might not have shattered the enemy, but it would have probably weakened the Ottomans to such a point that they could not pursue the campaign.

Unfortunately for the Persians, Durmish Khan intervened, insisting that the armies of Islam did not attack foes unprepared for battle. This may indeed have been news to the *Qizilbash*, who raided, plundered, slaughtered, and burned without mercy, but Ismail was persuaded, declaring, "I am not a *caravanserai* [roadside inn] thief…Whatever is decreed by Allah will occur."[47]

Such sentiments may have been gallant, but it meant Selim was allowed to line his artillery and shield them from cavalry charges with wagons joined by heavy chains, making them all but impervious to attack.

---

[47] Farrokh, p.24.

A monument on the site of the battlefield

Accounts of the battles vary, but it is possible to generally reconstruct the course of the conflict through knowledge of Ottoman and Safavid battle tactics and the sources where they agree. The Ottoman army was drawn into three groups: Janissaries with muskets in the center, with *sipahis* on the flanks (Hasan Pasha on the right and Hadim on the left). The artillery would have been behind them on elevated ground. Mortars would have been mounted on the wagons. Selim and his household cavalry, along with whatever reinforcements were present, would be positioned at the rear.

The battle almost certainly opened with a deafening cannon salvo that unsettled the cavalry on both sides. Then the Janissaries in the center would have advanced first, confident that their firepower would disperse counterattacking *Qizilbash*. This, however, proved not to be case, as the Persian center, with Ismail at its head and fighting personally, repelled the advance.

Both *sipahi* flanks then rode forth to cover the Janissaries' withdrawal, and at this point the Safavid flanks then entered the fray. The fighting was savage and chaotic, and at one point, Selim hoped to end the battle by sending his champion *sipahi* to challenge the Shah. However, upon sighting the warrior, Ismail charged and beheaded him without hearing the challenge. The *Qizilbash* fought fiercely, but at length Ismail realized that the Ottoman force was too strong to break and withdrew, but without conceding the field. He needed to consider another approach. The Ottoman force did not pursue, probably disorientated and in need of regrouping.

The fanatical ardour of the *Qizilbash*, especially after seeing the heroism of their leader, seemed to be having some effect on the enemy, and Ismail no doubt felt that victory was still within his grasp. As a result, instead of retreating in good order, he divided his forces into two groups and attacked the extreme Ottoman flanks, hoping that they would collapse upon the Janissaries and rout them. Ismail led the right flank personally, and both *sipahi* groups did give way, but the center remained firm, due to artillery on the hill behind them delivering crippling blows. Selim himself did not enter the fight, instead regarding the battle from the hilltop. He no doubt watched the decimation of the *Qizilbash* by his artillery with cool gratification.

The horrific end of the battle was described by Caterino Zeno, the Venetian ambassador to the Persian court: "The monarch [Selim], seeing the slaughter, began to retreat, and to turn about, and was about to fly, when Sinan, coming to the rescue at the time of need, caused the artillery to be brought up and fired on both the janissaries [sic] and the Persians. The Persian horses hearing the thunder of those infernal machines, scattered and divided themselves over the plain, not obeying their riders' bit or spur anymore, from the terror they were in ... It is certainly said, that if it had not been for the artillery, which terrified in the manner related the Persian horses which had never before heard such a din, all his forces would have been routed and put to edge of the sword."[48]

Despite the horrendous slaughter, the *Qizilbash* attacked again and again, at one point even reaching the line of artillery before being repelled. The *coup de grace* was delivered by Hadim Sinan, who had rallied the *sipahi* and attacked Ismail's flank. The counterattack was so powerful that Ottoman troops entered and plundered the Safavid camp, capturing the Safavid treasury and one of the Shah's wives.

At this point, Ismail had no choice but to concede the field. He went to the top of a hill and sounded the retreat, but to his dismay, only 300 warriors rallied to him.[49] Abd –al –Baqi Yazdi was slain, along with Mohammed Khan, Husayn Beg Shamlu, the head Shia cleric Sayyed Sharif al-Din Ali Shirazi, and Saru Pira Ustajlu

The cost to Selim had also been heavy. The ferocity and fanaticism of the *Qizilbash*, with

---

[48] Savory, p. 43.
[49] Farrokh, p.25.

Ismail himself leading them, would have overwhelmed a smaller army, but it was the size of Selim's army and his artillery that had saved the day. Ismail's failure to deploy artillery is all the more surprising when it is considered that he had used gunpowder weapons in previous battles.[50] It must be concluded that the Safavids chose not to use them on that occasion.[51] They did, however, learn the lesson, so they had adequate artillery for all future conflicts with the Ottomans, of which there would be many.

On September 14, 1514, two weeks after the battle, Selim entered Tabriz. The fall of the Safavid capital should have been catastrophic, but Ismail had fled from sight, no doubt gathering another army. Moreover, the *Qizilbash* had not even spared the capital in their scorched earth strategy, so Selim's army faced the prospect of wintering there without supplies and with little prospect of capturing the Shah. If the Ottomans remained, Safavid tribesmen could raid and harass the occupation force and, more seriously, the already tenuous Ottoman supply lines. Selim was also probably aware that another army led by Ismail might defeat him, especially if it was accompanied by artillery.

Thus, Selim reluctantly abandoned his plans for the conquest of Persia and left Tabriz just eight days after he entered it. He returned to Constantinople via the conquered Kurdish emirates of Eastern Anatolia, whose rulers he allowed to remain under Ottoman rule. He was not allowed to return unmolested, however; Georgian raiders harassed his army and continued to do so deep into Anatolia.

No peace treaty was concluded between Selim I and Ismail I. Indeed, none was possible, considering that they had declared each other heretics and beyond any respect that might be accorded them. Selim had nevertheless achieved his principle objective: the elimination of the Safavid menace in Anatolia. He had secured control of Eastern Anatolia, as well as northern Mesopotamia, and though Shiites remained within his borders, they were no longer a threat. Ottoman hegemony in Anatolia was secured.

Just as importantly for the Sultan, Selim had proven himself to his people, especially the military elite, and thereby consolidated his authority. There was at this time no major war with Europe (though raids into Christian territories were constantly undertaken), and the Sultan decided to use Ismail's defeat to conquer the Levant, then under the rule of the Egyptian Mamluk dynasty, which, like the Ottoman and Safavid aristocracies, was Turkoman in origin.

Ismail believed that Selim was preparing another campaign against him in 1516, so he entered into negotiations for an alliance with Mamluks. This was exactly what Selim wanted, for he could not obtain the approval of the Ulema for a war against a fellow Sunni monarch. If, however, such a leader aided Ismail, a heretical ruler, the Mamluk Sultan Tuman Bey II could be

---

[50] Ibid.
[51] Ibid.

declared a heretic as well.

Selim invaded Syria and defeated the Mamluks at the Battle of Marj Dabiq on August 24, 1516. By the end of January 1517, Selim had captured Mecca and sacked Cairo, the Egyptian capital.

This victory was important to the Ottoman Empire and to Selim personally for two reasons. First, the Ottomans now controlled most of the Eastern Mediterranean and the rich trade routes that stretched from Cairo to Aleppo in Syria, Algeria in Africa, and Mecca in Arabia. The exotic goods – much sought after by Europe – came from Asia through the markets of these lands, and the Ottoman state now had leverage against the trading powers of Europe, particularly Venice. Moreover, the Ottomans could now extend their influence into North Africa and the Indian Ocean. In this vein, Selim's son and successor, Suleiman the Magnificent (r. 1520–1566), would extend Ottoman rule over Tripolitania, Tunisia and Algeria, allowing him to disrupt European trade in the Mediterranean and raid its ports for slaves and booty. Moreover, it allowed the Ottomans to challenge Spanish power in the Wstern Mediterranean (with limited success). Control of Arabia and access to the Red Sea allowed them to challenge the Portuguese sea lanes to India (again, with limited success).

What was equally significant was that the Ottomans were now in possession of the three holy cities of Islam: Mecca, Medina and Jerusalem. This enhanced the dignity of Selim and his successors as protectors of the sacred places. Moreover, the last Sunni Caliph of the Abbasid dynasty, Al- Mutawakkil III (essentially a puppet of the Egyptian Sultans), was captured in Cairo and taken to Constantinople, where the elderly man was compelled to surrender the Sword and Mantle of Mohammed – symbols of his office – to Selim. The Sultan already claimed the authority of caliph but now it was formalised for the entire Islamic world to witness. He was now the ruler of all Sunnis wherever they were and, according to tradition, had the power to command them. His victory over the Mamelukes also deprived the Safavids of a potentially dangerous ally.

While the Battle of Chaldiran vastly increased the Ottoman Empire's power and elevated it to the status of a global power, the consequences of the defeat for Ismail and the Safavids, though not immediately apparent, were heavy nevertheless. After all, the defeat cost the Safavids an opportunity to weaken, if not destroy, the Ottoman state, though Persia itself largely preserved its territorial integrity. The *Qizilbash*, though weakened, were not destroyed, and they went on to win victories against the Uzbeks, who had launched an invasion of what is now Afghanistan in 1512.

The personal cost for Ismail, however, was great. He had risen to supremacy through the belief that he was the living voice of God, invincible and infallible. At Chaldiran, however, he had been humiliated by a heretic, someone cursed by God. For someone raised from infancy to believe that his relatives were the representatives of God on Earth, the humiliation must have been shattering. Although Safavid troops did aid the Mamluks and resist an Ottoman invasion of

Mesopotamia, Ismail himself never personally led an army against the Ottomans again. After Chaldiran, he began to give himself to pleasurable pursuits such as hunting[52] while leaving daily affairs of state to the Vakil. It was said that he drank alcohol, an activity considered shameful amongst Muslims.[53]

That said, Ismail was a prolific poet whose work is much esteemed in Iran. Before Chaldiran, his poetry was full of mystical self-aggrandizement, but by the end of his life it was often full of despair and melancholy. He wrote under the pen name Khatai ("Sinner" before dying in Tabriz in 1524.

Ismail's reign was by no means a failure, for he achieved much. He established, organised and stabilised a state that survives to this day, whereas the empire of his enemy Selim has passed into history.[54] He united Persia in a new and enduring faith, albeit by brutal and merciless means. Indeed, it has been difficult to find a dynastic founder who achieved so much in so little time. A notable failure, however, was his lack of control over the *Qizilbash*, and when he died, they fought over the succession.

The defeat at Chaldiran brought troubles to Persia from the Portuguese, whose sea lanes passed through the Persian Gulf on their way to the trading colonies in India. In 1507, the Portuguese commander Alfonso de Albuquerque conquered the island kingdom of Ormus (Hormuz), which lay in the entrance of the Persian Gulf. The Portuguese were now in a position to cut off Muslim trade with India and effectively isolate Persia from the West, and Ismail greatly desired cooperation with the European powers against the Ottomans. In 1515, the year after Chaldiran, Ismail, who did not possess a sizeable navy, had to acknowledge the Portuguese presence, yet another blow to his prestige as the invincible viceroy of God.

Diplomatically, however, the concession was not without is compensations. The Ottomans, rulers of Egypt and the Levant after 1517 sought to break the Portuguese stranglehold on trade, thus drawing Portugal and Persia into an alliance. This agreement brought cannons, muskets, and other firearms to the Persian army, thus empowering the Safavids in further conflicts with the Ottomans.

Through the Portuguese, Ismail also reached out to other European powers, and the Habsburg Emperor Charles V and Louis II, King of Hungary, both sent envoys to the Safavid court. In a 1523 letter written in Latin, the language of the Christians, Ismail urged a coordinated effort to destroy the Ottomans.[55] However, the Shah died the following year, and his successor, the boy Tahmasp I, became the center of a civil war which raged while Hungary succumbed to the Ottomans at the Battle of Mohacs in 1526.

---

[52] Farrokh, p.27.
[53] *The Cambridge History of Islam*, Part 1, By Peter Malcolm Holt, Ann K. S. Lambton, Bernard Lewis, p. 401.
[54] Modern Turkey cannot be identified with the Ottoman state, for the latter was not based on Turkish nationality.
[55] Farrokh, p.26.

In a way, the Battle of Chaldiran strengthened the Safavid state rather than weakened it. The young Shah and vicar of Allah, Ismail, along with his *Qizilbash* devotees, had naively crashed upon the world stage, believing that they were entitled to rule and needed no other help but God's. Chaldiran did not destroy the Safavids, but it awakened them to the reality of politics and government. They expanded the *Qurchi* regiments so as not to be dependent on the *Qizilbash*. They created a permanent artillery corps and established, as early as Ismail's reign, a unit of musketeers. A corps of *gholam* slave-soldiers was also created, and they, like the Janissaries, were dependent upon the monarch alone.

Reforms were also implemented in government. The office of Vakil was replaced by that of Grand Vizier, who presided over a Council of Ministers and was himself held accountable by a *vak'anevis* or deputy. The royal household was separated from the government with its own officials, chief of which was the *Nazir* or Court Minister, who was a conduit between the Shah and the government. This separation ensured that the executive would never dominate the palace.

These reforms served to consolidate the rule of the Safavids. In a second war with the Ottomans (1532–1555), Tahmasp I was defeated and had to concede lower Mesopotamia to Selim's son, Suleiman I the Magnificent. However, under Abbas I (r. 1588–1629), the Safavids briefly reconquered Mesopotamia and Eastern Anatolia. Abbas the Great is generally considered the most powerful of the Safavid monarchs. He also expanded into Caucasia and the Mughal Empire to the east, all feats which would have been impossible without the reforms of his predecessors.

The Ottomans proved to be the stronger empire but never conquered Persia, which was likely a logistical impossibility given the mountainous terrain and wide expanses of Persia. The closest the Ottomans came was in 1585, when they occupied Tabriz and held it for two decades, but it was onerous to supply the occupation force, especially when the population was Shiite. Abbas expelled the invaders and the Safavid-Ottoman border remained relatively stable until the Safavid dynasty was displaced in the 18th century.

Chaldiran indirectly benefited the Safavids economically, for the alliance with the Europeans and the Persian Gulf trade forced upon them by the Portuguese created a demand for Persian goods, including silks, textiles, leather, wool, precious stones, rugs, and tobacco. In 1622, Abbas I took Ormus from Portugal, thus regaining control of the Gulf trade. Persian commerce was strong enough to resist a trade embargo placed upon the Safavids by the Ottoman Sultan Mehmed III in 1603. However, in the 18th century the Safavid state declined and weakened, due largely to the control of Persian trade by the rising Dutch and British empires, as well as numerous costly wars.

For a time, something of Persia's former glory was restored under Nader Shah (r. 1736–1747), the "Napoleon of Persia."[56] who was not a Safavid but a former slave who deposed Abbas III (r.

1732–1736). Nader's own dynasty, the Afsharids, ruled Persia for the next 60 years, but even after the Afsharids, the prestige of the Safavid House was still so strong that the first ruler of the new Zand dynasty, Khaim Khan, found it necessary to install Ismail III, infant heir to the Safavids, as Shah to give his own reign legitimacy. When Ismail died in 1773, however, he was not replaced and the line of Safavid rulers ended forever.

Though the Safavid monarchy ended, the Persian monarchy did not. It survived for three more dynasties, until the deposition of Mohammad Reza Shah of the House of Pahlavi during the Iranian Revolution in 1979. Despite civil wars and foreign incursions, its borders and government have remained to this day relatively stable, due in no small part to the religion and government introduced by the Safavid dynasty.

The Ottoman dynasty held power longer, despite facing greater challenges. Since the central base of its power was in Rumelia (Ottoman Europe), it was forced to direct most of its attention west, where it confronted the technologically advanced states of Austria, Spain, Venice, Poland and Russia. Toward the end of the 17th century, it began to lose the struggle in the west while having to maintain a strong border presence against Persia. The conflict sent the empire into a decline from which it never recovered, whereas in Persia, stability was maintained. Persia successfully made the transition to constitutional monarchy in 1906, but the Ottoman attempt two years later failed, leading to the dissolution of the Ottoman Empire after World War I and the formation of the Turkish Republic.

Over 500 years after the battle, many modern scholars consider the Battle of Chaldiran a pivotal conflict that helped establish the Middle East as it exists today.[57] The outcome established the border between Iran and Turkey that remains largely unchanged to this day, and it drew Mesopotamia and the Levant into the Ottoman sphere. Thus, when the Ottoman Empire collapsed in the wake of World War I, Iraq was created from Mesopotamia and Syria, Lebanon, Israel, Palestine, and Jordan were carved out of the Levant. Almost all of these states came under the umbrella of the Sunni branch of Islam, where its adherents dominate (with the exception of Iraq, where the Shia still make up the majority). Conversely, in Iran, the Shia branch became the state religion and remains that way today.

Politics in the Middle East continue to be shaped by the Sunni-Shia conflict. Religious strife, mixed with ethnic, political, and economic differences, continue to affect many of the states in the region, such as in Iraq, where Iran continues to exert influence through the Shiite population established in Safavid times. Substantial Shia minorities also exist in Yemen, currently afflicted by civil war, and Iran continues to extend its sphere of influence into that country, as well as in Syria.[58] In October 2016, President of Turkey Recep Tayyip Erdogan declared that Turkey had a

---

[56] Michael Axworthy (2006), *The Sword of Persia: Nader Shah, from Tribal Warrior to Conquering Tyrant* I.B. Tauris, p. xvii.

[57] Akhilesh Pillalamarri, (August 21, 2014) "This 16th Century Battle Created the Modern Middle East", *The Diplomat*, https://thediplomat.com/2014/08/this-16th-century-battle-created-the-modern-middle-east/.

"historical responsibility" to combat Iranian-backed Shia militia in Iraq[59] and Syria, referencing the Ottoman-Safavid conflicts and the rise of the Persian Shiite state.

As this indicates, Turkey and Iran remain rivals for influence in the Middle East much like they were in the 16th century, and even in the modern secular Turkish Republic tensions remain between the majority Sunnis and the minority Shiites. The latter are not officially recognized by the Turkish government, and many fear that Erdogan's Sunni agenda might threaten their freedoms.[60] Iran remains unique as the only Muslim state with an overwhelmingly Shia majority (about 95 percent) and is again a theocracy, as in Safavid times, where the ruler, in modern times the Supreme Leader, is both the head of government and the religious head. The Constitution of the Islamic Republic of Iran recognises religious freedom in theory, though restrictions and discrimination is commonplace. For the leadership of Iran, Shia remains the authentic expression of Islam. Compare this belief with the growing Islamist sentiment in the Republic of Turkey. Constitutionally a secular state, its president has been observed turning it back to its Islamist roots. The *Jerusalem Post*[61] recently observed that Erdogan claims that Turkey is the leader of the Islamic (Sunni) world and that it needs to redefine itself in light of its imperial past. Supporters as well as critics of the Turkish leader often see him as a Caliph-like figure.[62]

Anti-Shia sentiment extends to its adherents in Sunni majority states across the world, including Indonesia, Malaysia and Pakistan. ISIS, which is a Sunni group, has led to a rise in Shia militias fearing persecution by the group and their sympathizers. The religious and political divide engendered by Chaldiran is still very much present.

If Ismail I had won the Battle of Chaldiran, it is likely that Iran and not the Ottoman Empire would have been the dominant power in the Middle East. Indeed, it is conceivable that the Ottoman Empire would have been destroyed entirely, and the Shia Safavids might then have gone on to dominate the Muslim world. It is no exaggeration then to suggest that the Middle East is the way it is because of Chaldiran.

---

[58] George Friedman & Kamran Bokharu (June 29, 2017), "5 maps that explain the modern Middle East", *Mauldin Economics,* https://www.mauldineconomics.com/editorial/5-maps-that-explain-the-modern-middle-east.

[59] "Erdogan: we have a historical responsibility in Iraq". *Aljazeera*, October 19 2016 https://www.aljazeera.com/news/2016/10/erdogan-historical-responsibility-iraq-161018133432623.html.

[60] Patrick Cockburn, "Turkish Shias in fear of life on the edge", *Independent,* October 6 2013, https://www.independent.co.uk/news/world/europe/turkish-shias-in-fear-of-life-on-the-edge-8862645.html.

[61] Robert Ellis, November 8, 2019 (written January 25, 2019), https://www.jpost.com/Opinion/The-new-caliph-578607.

[62] Jamie Dettmer (October 27, 2015), "Critics, even supporters say: Erdogan is the man who would be Caliph", *Voa* https://www.voanews.com/europe/critics-even-supporters-say-erdogan-man-who-would-be-caliph.

Online Resources

Other books about the Middle Ages by Charles River Editors

Other books about the Battle of Chaldiran on Amazon

Other books about the Ottomans on Amazon

Further Reading

Abou-El-Haj, Rifa'at Ali (1984). The 1703 Rebellion and the Structure of Ottoman Politics. Istanbul: Nederlands Historisch-Archaeologisch Instituut te İstanbul.

Ahmad, Feroz. The Young Turks: The Committee of Union and Progress in Turkish Politics, 1908–1914, (1969).

Aziz Basan, Osman, Great Seljuks, Taylor & Francis, 2010.

Babinger, Franz, Mehmed the Conqueror and his time, Princeton University Press, 1992.

Bein, Amit. Ottoman Ulema, Turkish Republic: Agents of Change and Guardians of Tradition (2011) Amazon.com

Bonner, Michael, et al., Islam in the Middle Ages, Praeger Publishers, 2009.

Cleveland, William L, A History of the Modern Middle East, Westview Press, 2000.

Erickson, Edward J. Ordered to Die: A History of the Ottoman Army in the First World War (2000) Amazon.com, excerpt and text search

Floor, Willem (2001). Safavid Government Institutions. Costa Mesa, California: Mazda Publishers. ISBN 978-1568591353.

Goodwin, Jason, Lords of the Horizons, Vintage books, 1999.

Howard, Douglas A, A History of the Ottoman Empire, Cambridge University Press, 2017.

Kafadar, Cemal, Between Two Worlds: The Construction of the Ottoman State, University of California Press, 1995.

Karlsson, Ingmar, Turkiets historia, Historiska media, 2015.

Karpat, Kemal H. The Politicization of Islam: Reconstructing Identity, State, Faith, and Community in the Late Ottoman State. (2001). 533 pp.

Kunt, Metin İ. (1983). The Sultan's Servants: The Transformation of Ottoman Provincial Government, 1550-1650. New York: Columbia University Press. ISBN 0-231-05578-1.

Maalouf, Amin, Korstågen enligt araberna, Alhambra, 2004.

Mango, Cyril A, The Oxford History of Byzantium, Oxford University Press, 2002

McCaffrey, Michael J. (1990). "ČĀLDERĀN". Encyclopaedia Iranica, Vol. IV, Fasc. 6. pp. 656–658.

McCarthy, Justin. The Ottoman Peoples and the End of Empire. Hodder Arnold, 2001. ISBN 0-340-70657-0.

McKay, John P., et al., A History of World Societies, Bedford/St Martins, 2014.

Mikaberidze, Alexander (2015). Historical Dictionary of Georgia (2 ed.). Rowman & Littlefield. ISBN 978-1442241466.

Peirce, Leslie (1993). The Imperial Harem: Women and Sovereignty in the Ottoman Empire. Oxford: Oxford University Press. ISBN 0-19-508677-5.

Runciman, Steven, The Fall of Constantinople, Cambridge Press, 1969.

Savory, Roger (2007). Iran Under the Safavids. Cambridge: Cambridge University Press.

Tezcan, Baki (2010). The Second Ottoman Empire: Political and Social Transformation in the Early Modern World. Cambridge: Cambridge University Press. ISBN 978-1-107-41144-9.

Uyar, Mesut & Edward J. Erickson, A Military History of the Ottomans, Praeger Publishers, 2009.

Villads Jensen, Kurt, Korståg: européer i heligt krig under 500 år, Dialogos, 2017.

Yves Bomati and Houchang Nahavandi,Shah Abbas, Emperor of Persia,1587-1629, 2017, ed. Ketab Corporation, Los Angeles, ISBN 978-1595845672, English translation by Azizeh Azodi.

Free Books by Charles River Editors

We have brand new titles available for free most days of the week. To see which of our titles are currently free, click on this link.

Discounted Books by Charles River Editors

We have titles at a discount price of just 99 cents everyday. To see which of our titles are currently 99 cents, <u>click on this link</u>.

Made in the USA
Las Vegas, NV
08 May 2022

48486577R10033